D1742709

THE BRIEF PRESENCE OF AN ABSENT GRANNY

WHEN I WAS A GIRL

To Beryl,

Best wishes. Monica

MONICA MATTERSON

The Brief Presence of an Absent Granny

Story and illustrations Copyright © 2014 by Monica Matterson
The right of the author to be identified as the author of this
work has been asserted in accordance with the
Copyright, Designs and Patents Act 1988.

First Published in 2015 by
Oxford eBooks Ltd.
Registered office
112 Poplar Grove, Kennington,
Oxford, OX1 5QP, UK

www.oxford-ebooks.com

All rights reserved. No part of this publication may be
reproduced, stored in a retrieval system, or transmitted, in any
form or by any means, electronic, mechanical, photocopying,
recording or otherwise, without the prior permission of the
copyright owners.

ISBN 978-1-908387-92-9 (Paperback)
ISBN 978-1-908387-95-0 (Hardback)
ISBN 978-1-908387-93-6 (ePUB)
ISBN 978-1-908387-94-3 (Kindle)

Oxford eBooks

Contents

Dedication

This book is dedicated to my grandsons, with much love.

Being referred to as 'Absent Granny', although I do enjoy the apt definition, it sometimes causes regrets that I have missed out on your childhood and so may lack a certain bond.

To try to make amends, I have put down these snippets for you in hope that you may enjoy them one day in the future.

Love Gran.

Early Days

It was Bonfire night, November the fifth in the year 1926, when I was born at a little house called Glenholme in Northgate, Hunmanby, Yorkshire.

My parents, Phyllis and John Edward Johnson were not wealthy at all but comfortable enough, they christened me 'Monica' which they thought stylish and different. So it was, in a village of Agnes's, Lizzies and Fredas but I have always disliked it, thinking the name cissy but I was not given a second one to choose from.

At that time, only a few houses in the village had running water or electricity and very few cars passed through. Our water came from a deep well and was pumped up by hand from a cast-iron pump at the side of the earthenware sink with its thick wooden draining board. Drinking water was from a village pump nearby.

The only form of heating was from the coal fire in the living room or the monstrous iron contraption for cooking on – the Kitchen Range! The fire inside heated large brass-knobbed ovens and a tank of water at the side and from somewhere amongst the chimney soot there protruded levers to open up the dampers to heat the ovens, and hooks to hang the kettle and cauldrons on. This monster had to be cleaned of soot and ashes every day, then polished with "Zebo" to keep it gleaming.

Coal dust and smoke soon begrimed the walls, windows and furniture making it necessary to Spring Clean when winter was over. The chimney sweep arrived on his bicycle, furniture was covered with sheets and everyone went outside to watch for the brush to appear from the chimney-top. After that, the walls were given a fresh coat of "distemper" – a lumpy version of emulsion, mixed from a powder with water. The only colours I remember were cream or white. Indoor paintwork was always brown, sometimes grained to look like oak, but still a dreary brown.

The iron bath was in the kitchen, the board covering served as a work surface until bath night, then it had to be filled with pans and jugs of hot water from the range. The toilet was an 'earth closet' in a wooden shed too far down the garden to be termed a 'convenience', so an enamel chamber pot was kept under the kitchen sink for any emergencies.

Upstairs was icy cold most of the time although there was a small fireplace in each bedroom – you had to be very poorly to warrant a fire being lit.

The earliest recollection I have was, at about two years old, being put outside in my pram and becoming bored. Thinking that if I jumped up and down a bit the pram would move…it did – it tipped over backwards! Screams soon brought me some attention.

Father was the proud owner of a "cat's whisker" radio. This modern invention was a large black Bakelite box the size of three small television sets with a face full of dials, knobs and switches which when twiddled issued forth ear-piercing squeals, whistles and clicks. Occasionally there was music, and the BBC news.

Mother owned a dog. This snappy, spoilt, jealous little black and tan Pekingese called "Nannette" took every pedigree, neurotic, opportunity to bite me, whereupon, I got the blame for teasing it and the dog got the sympathy. A mutual dislike developed between us. So I was given a pet of my own, a pretty white Angora rabbit. I felt sorry for it having to be in a cage all day, so I tried to take it for a ride in the doll's pram and clothes. It was not impressed, it leapt out and took refuge in the hedge. Two very angry parents spent the evening catching it.

After a few more unsuccessful attempts to 'train' it, several times forgetting to feed it and certainly no enthusiasm about the cleaning out routine, I went out one day to find the cage empty, oh dear! Had I left the door open?! Parental decisions had been made – they had given my pretty rabbit away. At three and a half years old I was not being responsible enough for them! So, back to the dog. She grudgingly tolerated the indignity of being dressed in dolls clothes and pushed about in the pram, until I over-insisted she lay on her back. That's when I got the biggest bite.

Early on Monday mornings at 'Glenholme,' a rosy-cheeked, round, cheerful village lady arrived wearing a coarse apron (sackcloth). She helped with the washing.

To keep me out of the way of all the boiling water, they sat me in the big wicker clothes basket with the clothes pegs and a Bakelite mug to have endless fun with!

The neighbouring children were considered too rough for me to play with. On the few occasions that I ventured to the front gate on my three-wheel Fairy cycle to watch them playing, I met with a barrage of stones. It was the broken dripping jar that cut my head and tumbled me into the bushes that, from then on , kept me in the back garden. It was safer digging up worms for the Rhode-Island Reds and White Wyandotte hens. They didn't seem to mind too much being chased and picked up!

Father

Born December 6th 1898, the eldest of a family of five. As a young child he was made blind in one eye whilst playing with a spinning top, and it had to be replaced with an artificial one. At seventeen years old, during the 1914-1918 first world war, he joined the Royal army Medical Corps and was sent out to France, to the trenches as a stretcher-bearer rescuing the wounded to bring them to the field hospital. Conditions in the trenches were appalling; wet, cold, muddy, insanitary and in the line of battle. As well as bombs and constant gunfire there were the feared mustard and tear-gas bombs which burnt the skin and affected the lungs. He was invalided out of the army with severely damaged lungs.

During his long convalescence and rehabilitation back in England he received training to become a master shoemaker in Sheffield where he met Phyllis Nora Palmer. They married in 1920 when he was 21 and she only 19 and lived, at first in Filey before moving to Hunmanby where he had a workshop. Until they moved, he had walked the three miles each way every day to his work in all weathers to make the special shoes and boots for people with odd shaped feet. The customer would stand on a piece of brown paper while he drew around their feet. From that blueprint he produced the pairs of lovely hand-stitched shoes of fine leather, mostly for gentlemen.

The nearby girls' boarding school kept him busy with repairs. I do not remember much about him except that he was very strict, but kind with a great sense of humour, and a natural gentleman who was frequently ill. I never really knew him.

Mother

She mostly seemed to share similar qualities with the dog - bossy, snappy, spoilt and demanding but was capable of being caring and affectionate too. She ran the shoe shop attached to the house, and the household with a fastidiousness that was far too stringent for me, or anyone else to conform with. When she said "My nerves are bad today!" I kept as far away as possible to avoid being in trouble. Mostly, I was afraid of her, other times I was smothered by her overprotectiveness and later we then seemed to disapprove of each other most of the time.

Dad, Grandma, Mum, Grandad, Monica - 1927
Note "Dickie" seat at rear of car.

Dressed for the beach! The Barriers, Filey 1927
Father, Grandad, Grandma, Mother and Monica

No deck chairs today, dig yourself a hole!

Grandma Palmer showing her bloomers!
And mother with me in pram. 1927.
Note old bathing machines.

Grandma and Grandad Palmer testing the water, 1927

The 1930s

At four years old, it was exciting to move to a large house in Hunmanby. Church Hill House stood on a corner at the top of a hill near the middle of the village and, of course, near the church. We now had electric lights, an electric cooker as well as the kitchen range, and a bathroom.

The only toilet was still outside, but not so far away. It was across the yard instead of down the garden, brick-built with a wooden box construction, seat with lid and a large bucket underneath – far superior! Once a week it was emptied by Harry Gash, whose shaggy, forlorn old nag pulled a galvanised tank on wheels from house to house. Access to this foetid bucketful was by a small trapdoor in the wall nearest the street. We rarely saw him come; he was, in polite terms "The Midnight Express!"! Toilet tissue such as we have today was unknown. The next best thing was a roll or box of *Jeyes lavatory paper* – stiff, crackly and unkind, and seemed a luxury. Families hung up their last years' almanac on a string and we spent our evenings cutting up the daily newspaper into squares and threading it. The rest of the newspaper was used for lighting the fire next morning and for making spills. There was a canister of nasty pink carbolic powder to sprinkle down the hole after use, this was considered to be hygienic, so too was the fly-paper dotted with black corpses that had been lured by this deadly strip as it hung from a spidery beam. The 3 inch gap under the door let in the only source of light and a discouraging draft.

This house had a bathroom of sorts. Enormous taps dominated the spacious cast iron bath with eagle's-claw feet in the long narrow room. Being a recent innovation, and the plumbing not yet thought out, the cold water still had to be pumped up from the cistern in the cellar and the hot carried up by the bucketful. I thought we had gone up in the world.

Drinking water had to be fetched in buckets as needed from the communal *parish pump* which was fortunately just outside our big wooden gates known as 'broad doors'.

THE VILLAGE PUMP 1930

This pump was later replaced by *town water* which gushed aggressively from a lion's mouth on a cast iron pedestal.

At street level, the front part of the house was the shoe shop that mother ran while father only had to walk half way down the hill to his workshop.

Then arrived our first housemaid - Kitty, so I thought we must be rich! "Not so", I was frequently reminded – "and if you keep on scuffing your shoe toes and leaving your crusts you'll have us all in the workhouse scrubbing floors with only stale bread and water for your meals!"

This prospect frightened me profoundly, especially when my shoes were inspected every evening for signs of stone-kicking and puddle jumping. I was always in trouble for something that I thought trivial.

Kitty was just fourteen years old, the eldest of a large family, so she was considered very fortunate to have found a 'position' as soon as she had finished all the education she was likely to get. It meant too, that her family would have one less mouth to feed plus some share of the five shillings (25 pence) a week wages.

Wearing her morning uniform of blue cotton dress, coarse apron and mop-cap, she cleaned out ashes, polished the kitchen range, swept, dusted, polished furniture and scrubbed the steps under mother's critical supervision, which she said, made her tremble, especially when dusting the ornaments. When the mid-day washing up was finished, Kitty put on her afternoon uniform – a brown cotton dress and frilly cream apron and cap, so that she could serve afternoon tea in style to callers or indulge any light duties. She was very kind to me; we were allies – we shared mother's wrath all too often.

The House. 1931

Because it stood on a hill, the cellars were accessible from ground level at the back, and a flight of stone steps led up to the back door. (The basement cellars are now a garage). The first cellar room housed a vast cistern or well to store the rainwater from the roof. A thick round wooden lid covered the frightening, eerie echoing blackness below.

My swing hung in the doorway. Many circus acrobatics, bumps and skinned knees happened here. Past the swing and straight on was the coal hole. The coal-man tipped his sacks through the man-hole up on the front pavement down to fill this small black room. I didn't go near there or any of the other mysterious storage rooms with dark shadows, spiders and no doubt mice.

The largest cellar-room had a flagstone floor, windows, a fireplace and sink so possibly it was once the servants' quarters when the house was first built sometime between 1785 and 1875.

Monday

The dreaded Monday Washday happened here.

Early in the morning, Kitty set to work. The brick-built copper in the corner was filled with water pumped up from the cistern and bucketed across from the sink. Nearby stood the chopping block and axe to chop sticks to start the fire to burn the coal to heat the water to boil the sheets and towels and wash the clothes! I never did understand the procedures that involved all these wooden troughs, galvanised tubs, dolly-pegs, copper sticks, blue bags and buckets of starch before the mangling could begin.

The MANGLE! A mighty contraption of fancy floral cast ironwork surrounds two tree-trunk sized wooden rollers which took more brute force than enthusiasm to wind the heavy linen sheets through as you turned the wheel. Midst a cloud of steam, mother and Kitty toiled for most of the day. Then, when the clothes line was fluttering in the cobbled yard all the soapy water was thrown across the cellar floor and Kitty scrubbed it on hands and knees. Is this what growing up means? What an awesome thought! Perhaps being a child is not so bad after all – in spite of constant scoldings.

Tuesday

- was for ironing! Three heavy flat irons were set close to the fire to heat up, then with an iron holder (unevenly and reluctantly knitted by me as a Christmas present) take up an iron and spit on it on the bottom; if it sizzles it is hot enough! Ironing was done on the kitchen table protected by a piece of sheet over an old blanket - no ironing boards yet!

The finished clothes were hung over a tall wooden clotheshorse in front of the fire to air – no airing cupboards either! The only warm place to sit and read was on the floor between the fire and this 'steam-laundry' it was peaceful there!

In summer, a neighbour, Miss Codling did her washing outside in the communal yard shared by three houses. She was thin, bony, ancient and wore a weird floral shift – I thought she might be a witch.

 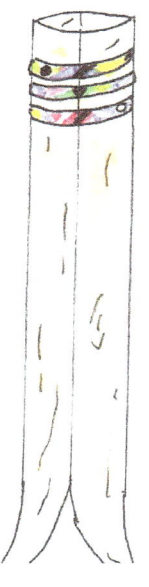 Our clothes pegs in that era were hand made. The menfolk of the travelling Romanies would take about one inch diameter small branches from the hedgerows and cut them into 4 – 5 inch lengths, then split them down the middle and shape rounded points at the split ends. The next step was to cut discarded tin cans into narrow strips and wind round the top end and securing with tin tacks to stop the peg from splitting further. About twice a year the ladies hawked them round the villages in baskets together with their 'lucky' heather. Cross their palms with silver, and you got your fortunes told also.

Wednesday

Bedroom day! Fitted carpets were still an item of the future. There were carpet squares to put on top of the patterned linoleum, but you were lucky to find one to completely fit a room. Every household had lots of hand-pegged rag rugs, a winter occupation for using up time and your old skirts and blouses. These all had to be taken down two flights of stairs, hung on the clothesline to be frantically beaten and brushed then taken back again. With neighbours in close proximity you had to make an issue of this to avoid being thought a 'slut'!

Our 'en suite bathroom' was the marble-topped washstand with its matching set of flower-patterned china wash basin, water jug, soap dish, toothbrush holder and, of course the chamber pot for under the bed. An enamel bucket with a lid for the waste water completed the set. Unless you were really poorly, the washing water was always freezing cold as were the bedrooms, so not a lot of time was wasted washing and dressing in the mornings. The bathroom was only for bathing.

Thursday

The local farmer delivered our milk every day, fresh from his cows, creamy and untreated, and ladled into our jugs straight from one of the two buckets he carried on the wooden yoke across his shoulders. On Thursdays though he also brought fresh curds and whey (nowadays known as Cottage Cheese).

Two basins were left out for it as today is baking day.

Enough bread was made to last a week, the two enamel washing-up bowls of dough being set on the hearth to rise while the rest of the baking was being done. There were scones, Sally Lunns (a kind of teacake), several Yorkshire curd tarts, and sponge cakes.

Kitty was kept busy with washing up and fetching coal to keep the ovens hot enough for this day–long marathon while I helped by licking out the bowls and scrounging the pastry trimmings. The electric oven was thought to be too new-fangled to be trusted.

Friday

Yet more housework. Polishing brasses and the every-day knives and forks. Cutlery was not stainless steel as it is today, and had to be frequently rubbed very hard with a paste made of methylated spirits and a bright pink powder with an unpleasant smell. There were sticks to be chopped and buckets of coal to bring up from the cellar.

Saturday

Even on Saturday, Kitty came to work, Father went down to his workshop and Mother was busy in the shop until six o'clock and often until ten o'clock in summer.

After lunch, I waited patiently to be given my 'Saturday Penny'. I was not allowed to ask or hint for it or was kept waiting longer. It was agonising wondering if they had forgotten or I had not deserved it this week.

Sunday

The traditional Sunday dinner of roast beef and Yorkshire puddings frequently ended in tears when it came to being force-fed with cabbage or sprouts before being sent off to Sunday school to give them a bit of peace. The lovely twelfth century church was only a few yards away and the well-attended class was strictly governed by a small roly-poly lady (Mrs Hargreaves) with hair like steel wool, tightly pulled back, plaited and coiled into a bun - she seemed very old to me. The atmosphere was always hushed and tense - "Because, dear children, you are in God's house and He sees all you do." A frightening prospect for a six-year old! It was most uncomfortable kneeling on the lumpy hassocks and often the bare floor. The prayers seemed endless, but you dare not fidget, so AMEN came with a great relief, and was voiced with gusto.

Usually, there followed *All things bright and beautiful* accompanied by Mrs Hargreaves on an ancient harmonium with a mind of its own. Occasionally, the vicar himself (Canon Brooke-Jackson) took the class. He was small, round and jolly and held us in awe with stories. He also had a beautiful garden where we were invited to pick snowdrops from his shrubbery. In summer there were tea parties followed by running races on the lawn. This sounds very tame now, but this was all part of village life before modern sophistication crept in.

On fine Sundays, I would be taken for a sedate walk along the country lanes, dressed in my Sunday best. I can remember a white rabbit-skin coat, hat and hand-muff on a cord, worn with sensible brown calf lace-up shoes topped with leather gaiters buttoned to the knees with the button-hook.

There was no chance of kicking a stone or climbing a tree, I was usually having a nature lesson from Father.

One time, though, he took me to a chaffinches nest just as the chicks were hatching from the eggs. He had been observing the nest for weeks and managed to time it right for me – I was quite impressed.

School 1930-34

There were no play-groups or nursery schools then, at least not in a small village. So as soon as I turned four years old, I started at the infants' school at the bottom of the hill. Most days, I was chased home by a gang of local kids. I now think they must have classed me as stuck-up and over privileged because I wore clean socks and didn't have a runny nose or head-lice!

I soon became very good at running – especially up hill, although there was Father's workshop for refuge half way up if things got nasty.

On the first day there, I was given a penny by the headmaster (Mr Bray) for identifying a robin. School didn't seem so bad after all. On the next day, and numerous other days, I was sent behind the blackboard for talking. At first, we wrote on slates, with a sponge on a string tied to one corner, but the slate pencils broke into fragments when dropped, which was too often. For all lessons, we sat in rows at tip-up desks and the penalties for talking, fidgeting or not facing the front varied only slightly. "Hands on heads and eyes shut!" that was most frequent – "Stand on seats!" that caused a commotion, but "Stand on seats, hands on heads and eyes closed!" was the ultimate discomfort. It seemed an eternity before normal positions were thankfully resumed.

Many of the children walked up to two miles each day from the outlying farms. I was not much liking the farm boys as they always smelt strongly of sour milk and manure which emanated from their thick ginger-brown, knee-length corduroy trousers and heavy boots which trod on my feet during the dreaded, weekly dancing class.

Just before each play time, trays of mugs of Horlicks were brought into each class room. It was hot, thick and frothy, cost threepence per week and was very comforting in contrast to the playground. This was an area of half asphalt and half gravel causing tearfully sore knees in the daily rough and tumble. Courage and desperation were needed to use the block of obnoxious outside toilets – old earth closets, where the wind, rain or snow blew straight in.

Some of the children played marbles around the drain gratings, but I couldn't understand the rules. The girls bounced balls to a variety of actions and chants, they skipped and chanted, and played chanting circular games while the boys fought and kicked footballs through the girls games.

The 'three R's' were easy, but having to learn to knit socks on four needles, at seven years old, was not. Being a dedicated chatterbox is not good for concentration, and an angry Miss Cully loudly brought to my attention that I was now knitting on three needles instead of four… "stand on seat, hands on head and eyes closed!" she barked. I stood, I heard the bell ring for the end of afternoon school, and I heard everyone leave as the class was dismissed, but no-one told me to get down and I dare not disobey. Perhaps only ten minutes passed, but it seemed like hours. "What if everyone has gone home and locked up?" I thought, "No, she'll come back… or perhaps she's forgotten me." More time passed, it was very quiet with no sound of anyone about – I was very frightened, so I opened my eyes and saw no-one, so I hopped down and ran the fastest yet up the hill, and I hadn't even been missed at home.

Near to Christmas, we all had to make calendars for our parents. Not often did we get to enjoy the power of scissors and glue! I carefully cut out some shiny stars, but that annoying lock of hair kept falling over my eyes and was becoming more of a nuisance each time I pushed it away with glued up fingers. "That's better!" I felt, putting down the scissors as the offending clump of hair fell across the desk, which unfortunately was on the front row. The look of disbelief on the teacher's face was quite memorable as was the tanning with the back of the hairbrush on my bottom when I got home.

Perhaps if I hadn't misjudged the amount I cut off, or had cut it straight they might not have noticed and there would not have been such an unsightly tuft for several weeks!

In a village in the 1930s it was quite safe to wander anywhere, the 'traffic' was mainly horse and cart or a traction engine. At seven years old, I had plenty of friends and often walked alone to visit farm friends (girls were ok – they didn't wear smelly corduroys) who lived two miles away up a long track through some woods. No one seemed to worry if we roamed far afield as there were very few cars about and you usually recognised everyone you saw.

It was quite normal to play on the road. One of the street games was 'boolers'. A booler, or 'bowler' was an iron hoop bowled along, usually in the gutter, guided by a metal rod with a hook on the end – or with just a stick. It was mostly a boys toy, which sounds very tame these days.

Whips and tops traditionally came into the shops at Easter. There were two types of top. One was cone-shaped, steady and reliable, with a flat upper surface on which you chalked coloured circles to make a pattern whilst spinning. It very soon smudged, so you washed it off and started again, but being too impatient to let it dry properly, it looked a mess and had to be held in front of the fire to dry. The decoration was important and competitive!

The other type of top was the 'window-breaker', it was undecorated, lively, and frequently lived up to its name when a good lash with the whip made it unpredictable and dangerous, that is how my father was blinded when a young boy.

my whip had leather Bootlace not string

WINDOW BREAKER

Boys had pea-shooters, a metal tube through which they spat dried peas at the girls. They also had cap guns, cap bombs and potato guns. In the autumn we all played conkers.

Next door to us lived the Garbutts. One day I swapped all of my lead farmyard animals for one of their son's tatty old books just so that I could paint its uncoloured pictures. Mother was greatly displeased, and I soon regretted it, but I had to keep the book and often missed my farmyard.

Next door to them was Mr Marshalls' grocery shop. He was round and jolly and everyone called him 'Tot'. The shop was small and dark with a low beamed ceiling and smelt strongly of a mixture of camphor, paraffin, coffee, smoked bacon and fresh bread. Biscuits, a limited, boring selection were displayed in large square tin boxes with glass lids and were weighed out on the old scales with brass weights. Sugar came out of a hundredweight sack, shovelled onto the scales, then tipped onto the centre of a square of blue 'sugar paper'. After a few deft folds, a shake or two and more folds, you had as neat a bag of sugar as you now have from the supermarket.

Several blends of tea were stored in ornately painted gold and brown canisters on the side shelf along with the coffee which was ground for you as required. Butter and lard stood on a marble slab in two foot cubes waiting to have one pound blocks cut off and patted into shape, then wrapped in greaseproof paper. There was a chair for the customer whilst waiting.

Whole sides of bacon hung, pig-shaped on hooks from the beams to be sliced on demand, neatly overlapped, folded and packaged. I had never heard of margarine.

Large glass jars full of sweets tantalised on a shelf behind the counter. There were acid drops, pear drops, aniseed balls, coconut mushrooms, Pontefract cakes, dolly mixtures and striped humbugs all for two pence a quarter (4oz).

'Kali' suckers, gobstoppers, liquorice shoelaces, cinder toffee and sherbet were only a halfpenny or a farthing each, but mostly considered 'rubbish' by mother and I was not allowed to buy them with my Saturday Penny. So, by the time I allotted the compulsory 'one for Mummy' and 'one for Daddy' of the more expensive 'non-rubbish' there would be very little left but to wait until next Saturday. Sometimes Tot would give me some of the slivers and some crumbs from the slab of Sharp's Toffee left in the tray after it had been cracked into lumps with the little brass toffee hammer. Other children at school seemed to have sweets every day! Sometimes a visiting uncle would give me sixpence, Grandma Mitton always gave me half a crown (2/6, now 12½ p) but I was not allowed to buy anything with it. It went straight to the Yorkshire penny bank on Monday morning! Then I could look forward to weekly comics – *The Rainbow* in which "Pip, Squeak and Wilfred" (a dog, rabbit and a penguin) had the most exciting adventures – all for 2d!

Tot lived in a pretty cottage across the cobbled yard beyond a stable where his sturdy white cart horse 'Kossack' and the dray were kept. One day each week he would load up the dray with provisions; bread, buns, biscuits, fruit, vegetables, tea, sugar and paraffin, then leaving his wife to tend the shop, back Kossack into the shafts and take to the road. Sometimes, in the summer he would take me with him. It felt very grand

"TOT" MARSHALL'S GROCERY SHOP
in 1932

33

sitting on the front amongst the boxes as the patient horse plodded slowly through the country lanes and up steep hills to the outlying villages which had no shops and infrequent public transport. Reighton, Speeton and Bempton were visited. The coastguard cottages at Speeton were at the highest point. There, Kossack usually had a brief rest, oats and water and I thought it was a great luxury to be given a leftover banana or a sticky bun before returning late in the afternoon from the slow, ten mile round plod. The poor old horse eventually pulled its last dray and died, whereupon Tot

bought himself a smart new brown Ford van with "Try our celebrated T" in bold gold letters across the back doors. While admiring it and trying to be polite, I ventured to ask him if the 'T' was for Tot, and was rewarded by a smart slap and scolding from mother for being so impudent. I couldn't understand it!

At about the same time, 1933/34, my Grandparents, who lived at Scalford, near Melton Mowbray, visited us in a new Vauxhall saloon – a huge black oblong box of a car, registration number MJ48. I was very impressed that Grandfather had bought a car with my initials on it and was very proud to be taken out in it for a picnic on Whitby Moors.

What a palaver that was! Why do grown-ups put on their work-a-day clothes, take hours making mountains of sandwiches, packing up scones, tarts, fruitcake, tinned fruit, cream and several flasks of tea? Then take so much time loading the big hamper fitted with cups, saucers and plates? And now, why does it take so long for them to change into their almost identical, striped silk dresses and straw hats while Father and Grandfather prowl impatiently in their best suits, polished shoes and Trilby hats?! "Have you put in those three tartan rugs?", "Ye-ees", "Have you got a handkerchief?", "Ye-ees!" At last we're off. Grandma complaining about the drafts, even when it's hot, and getting hysterical on every hill. Although the car is more modern, her and Mother still get out and walk up any steepish incline, partly because they don't trust Grandfather's gear changes and mostly because they are both too portly for the good of the car and he gets flummoxed when they scream if the car runs backwards under their weight as he fluffs a gear. Folkton Brow, Hackness Hairpins and Sutton Bank were guaranteed to bring on dramatic displays of tears, temper and screams of fear until we stopped to let them out, whether going uphill or down! No wonder it took so long to go anywhere.

Eventually, a suitable patch of grass is chosen among the heather and grandma goes off to prod it with her walking stick to test it for dampness, and scrutinise it for sheep or rabbit droppings. If it meets her approval, she waves the stick and shouts "Bring the things!" In her most authoritative manner she supervises whilst everyone else 'brings the things'.

'CHILPRUFE' VEST ALL WOOL.

FLEECY LINED 'LIBERTY' BODICE
WITH DETATCHABLE SUSPENDERS.

KNICKERS.

PETICOAT. 'ART' SILK.

A little girl cannot have a lot of fun dressed in a yellow knitted silk dress edged with swan's down worn over a woollen vest, liberty bodice, petticoat, voluminous knickers, white socks, sandals and a panama hat – especially when being watched over by your over-dressed adults on a bleak moor with not even a tree to climb. Sometimes there may be a shallow stream, but I must not wet my shoes or socks and taking them off was never mentioned. The men kept on their trilby hats or caps that set off their suits, waistcoats, starched collars and ties.

Sometimes, I played with June, the daughter of the local vet. Theirs was a large house with lots of garden and outhouses to explore. They employed two maids, but if we strayed into the kitchens we had to help with the chores. The sink, a shallow, glazed stone trough held a large round wooden washing up bowl like half a barrel. How I hated having to help to wash up! The tepid water was always grey and greasy with nasty bits lurking underwater from unscraped plates

There was no *Fairy Liquid* then, just soda crystals to help soften the water and redden your hands. Then the knives have to be cleaned, but they had a 'modern labour saving device' that you slotted the knives into, put in the same pink powder and turned a handle. More fun than at home. This house also proudly owned about the first indoor flush toilet in the village, but we had to use the unique relic of a 'family six-holer' in the garden, housed in what was once the front room of the gardener's cottage.

It had a well-scrubbed brick floor, broken windows, a wealth of spiders and served as our playrooms on a wet day!

On cold days we could thaw out by going in to see the gardeners in the vast greenhouse which was warmed by a coal-burning boiler feeding hot water through iron pipes running the length of it. On the pretext of admiring his plants we could absorb the dampness and geranium-scented warmth.

The Annual Show

For weeks beforehand, the whole village would be buzzing with plans and preparations of this important event, even at school. I cannot recount just how many times we had to write and re-write for the hand-writing competition:-

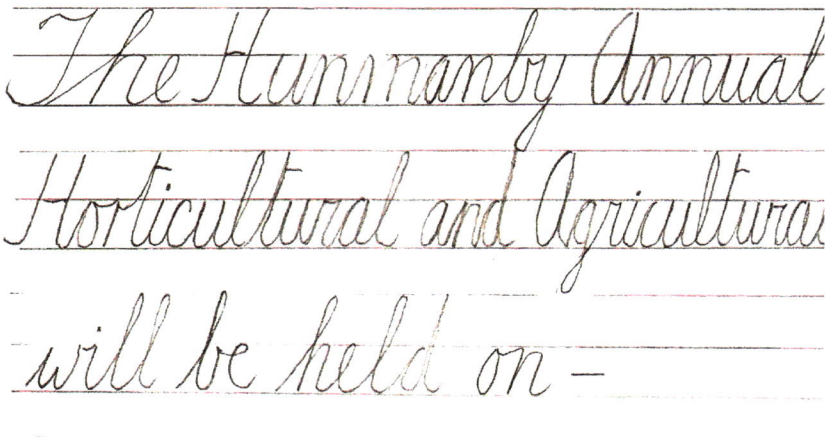

The Hunmanby Annual Horticultural and Agricultural will be held on —

It took many frustrating attempts to get it right enough to exhibit and I was very happy to receive second prize, 1/- (5 pence) on two occasions and also for knitting a scarf for my teddy bear. Almost everyone in the village put something in the show. One tent for children's wild flower arrangements, another for the adults garden flowers, while the marrows potatoes, onions and other seasonal vegetables were praised and criticised by their competitors in the next one. Then there were the cakes, jams and pickles, painting, embroidery, knitting, and not forgetting the handwriting. Now we come to the livestock, - with every tent having its own smells and sounds. Rows of pet rabbits sorted into their different breed, birds, dogs, cats, mice, guinea-pigs, ducks, hens and cockerels, all trying to look the most handsome.

Outside in the pens were sheep, cows and bulls. The patient shire horses had been sleekly groomed and their tails and manes plaited up with coloured braids, harnesses gleamed with jangling brasses. Some of them were pulling brewers' drays carrying their bolwer-hatted, aproned, 'whip in hand' drivers sitting straight in suspension.

The local band plays and the children skip around them. The merits of the new turnip cutters, ploughs and often new-fangled agricultural hardware are inspected and debated by a group of farmers shouting above the hissing of the polished traction engine and the shiny machines that have now got steam up in the corner. Further up the field, the girls from the Hall School give an elegant dancing display in their green brief silk togas - how I envied them them!

Later in the afternoon, it was compulsory that we children compete in the races. Being too afraid of going wrong, I avoided the sack race, egg and spoon and obstacle races, but the hundred yards sprint I was well practised at. We were all lined up, including two of the girls who always chased, but never caught me. The worst one, was tall, skinny, with protruding teeth, hair scraped back into one long pigtail and 'bottle' glasses held on with elastic, really ugly, - you know the sort! – I do still remember her name. Her mother was determined that her 'little darling' was going to win and stood behind her as the man with the flags shouted "Ready, steady, GO!" - she did,- her mother gave her a hearty push to help her on the way and she went flat on her face in the grass! She rose up bawling and sniffing – what a glorious moment, such was my pleasure, I almost forgot to run!!

The Fair came to Cross Hill In Hunmanby in the autumn. One shilling and sixpence seemed a fortune and brought many rides on chairoplanes, swing boats, cakewalk, and the carousel with the painted horses, and perhaps left enough for a penn'orth of chips and some 'scraps 'at the end. The loud jangling music of the steam

organ and flashing lights on the garish paintwork seemed magical.

Also, in winter time came the occasional visit of the man with the "Mysterious Magical Lantern Show" an exciting event held in the church hall! A box-like, tin contraption lit by an oil lamp, magnified distorted sepia images of animals onto a white sheet and sometimes, flickering, jerky moving 'comic' sequences had everyone laughing. Television was still a long way off.

Holidays 1930's

As we already lived near the seaside, mother didn't consider it necessary to have holidays, but I was taken to Torquay for a week when I was seven years old and to Bournemouth the following year. Grandma and Grandad took mother and me, but poor Dad had to stay behind to work and look after the shop. First we went down to Grantham by steam train, changing at Seamer and again at York where we caught the famous 'Flying Scotsman' into Grantham to be met by Grandad in the car for the remaining eighteen miles. The journey took all day but I enjoyed it. All next day would be spent driving down to Torquay - There were no motorways. We stayed in a large Victorian house, occupying a front room and two bedrooms and bought our own food for the landlady to cook and serve.

Mother and Grandma were more interested in looking around the big shops than going to the beach, so Grandad was usually left with keeping me amused. One day, I was really enjoying myself at high tide, dodging the waves on the steps in Torquay. Grandad read his paper in peace on a nearby seat, oblivious that I had badly misjudged a big wave and was now being stripped down to my knickers by some good lady with an awesome bosom. She 'tut-tutted' as she spread all my superfluous undergarments and silk dress out to dry on the wall, while I enjoyed the freedom of being dressed (or undressed) for the water.

I suspect that Grandad was too embarrassed to acknowledge ownership of me, as he kept well behind his paper until I was dressed again. Then he claimed me "Whatever you do, don't tell your mother or Grandma!" he winked as he bought me an ice-cream.

It was decided without my consent, that I must learn to swim, so was taken each day for an hour's lesson, so that mother and grandparents could relax in peace with their coffee and newspapers in the adjoining sun lounge. This, I was told had a special "Vita glass" roof and windows which let the ultra-violet rays through i.e., - sunbathing under glass! My lessons went well as long as they dragged me along on a rope attached to a rubber ring on each arm.

The problem arose on the last day when it was assumed that I should now be able to swim one length unaided, except for an occasional prod under the chest with a long pole – not likely!! Exhibiting my loudest displeasure, I gripped the side of the pool, too petrified to move. After refusing to oblige the cajoling instructors, I was forcibly removed from the pool and returned, in deep disgrace, to the bosoms of my family where I earned not the slightest sympathy, I had disturbed their leisure and wasted their money - ungrateful child! Grandad sneaked me an ice-cream.

On the Bournemouth holiday, I can remember feeding the red squirrels in the park and having to sit quietly in a deck-chair for what seemed hours, listening to a military band doing their best with *Poet and Peasant* or *Zampa*. Apart from the day when the conductor stepped backwards off his rostrum, I found this grown-up pastime tedious and boring. Occasionally we went to the beach but at no time can I remember that those two formidable ladies, mother and Grandma put themselves out to play with me.

One hot sunny evening I was hustled off to bed at 6:30 pm, curtains closed and strict instructions not to get out of bed. They were going out to a show on the pier, "The Crazy Gang" perhaps! I had dared to open a crack in the curtains just enough to read a comic by, when there was a gentle knock on the door. Again, forgetting instructions I hopped out and opened it. In the bright sunlight shone the faces of three smiling children, one pretty girl and two boys armed with toys and books. They were such a happy little family, we talked, read, and played until the fear of being caught dawned on me. I hadn't realised how lonely I was. Next day, we all rose early and met in the dining room for more chatter until I was found and scolded for talking to strangers - especially boys! They left that day and I never saw them again. It was not until over fifty years later that I found the letter that Paddy had written to me when I was nine. My mother obviously considered it a too shockingly dangerous liaison to even tell me about, and had kept it hidden. I found it after her death in 1970. I was very hurt, a polite reply was all it needed and I never saw the Christmas card he sent either!

28 Durham Rd.
North Harrow,
Middx.

30th. Dec. 1935.

My Dear Monica.

Just a note to say that I hope you got my Christmas card in time for Christmas.

See I have not forgotten you, even though it was a long time ago, I still remember you at Bournemouth, your pretty face.

Did you have a nice Christmas, I hope you did, because I like you, nearly above all the things, you look so pretty?

I hope you remember me, that boy at Bournemouth, and espicially that night at Bournemouth when I talked with you.

Please will you send me a letter all about yourself and your telephone number, if you have one, and please, I beg of you, will you send me a picture of your beautiful face.

A HAPPY NEW YEAR.

with all my love
My Monica,

Your loving friend

Love
xxx xxxxxx Paddy (Galvin) xxxxx xxxx

Grandma Mitton' - June 13th 1876-1966

This Grandma was very different to mothers' mother, she was plump, jolly, and very kind and loving. Grandfather Johnson had died when she was 46 years old and three years later she re-married a Harry Mitton at Sheffield. They moved to Bridlington, where she enjoyed running a succession of small boarding houses, always on the move to one bigger and better. I never knew what Harry did, he was always there sitting in his chair, in his suit and outsize gold watch and chain and didn't say much!

Grandma visited us by bus in Filey and Hunmanby and always gave me the vast sum of 2/6d as well as lovely birthday and Christmas presents, especially after father died. There was the fancy brush and comb set, fur gloves, leather writing case and first bicycle for my 16th birthday. Mother didn't approve of any of them, perhaps because they were generous.

If only I'd listened to her stories, and asked questions about her life, - but the family said she romanticised and made things up when she couldn't remember. I loved her just the same. As she got older and Harry died, she still wouldn't give up being a landlady - she loved looking after people. Then her houses became smaller, but she still took in a young man who came for a week's holiday and stayed several years under her wing. She was not careful with money and eventually in her late eighties, still very independent, was reduced to a rented room, having given away all her possessions to her friends and family. She was still jolly, I did ask her if she was ever lonely – "No, never. I have a lap full of memories!"

Most summers until I was ten, were spent at my grandparents, mother and father being too busy in the shop and workshop to worry about what I was up to. Uncle Fred often came to fetch me in his latest sports car, a three-wheel chain driven Morgan or a Singer. The journey from Hunmanby to Scalford took over five hours - that's if the radiator didn't boil over, or the "big end go" whatever that meant!

From left to right. Grandma Mitton, Grandma Palmer, Grandad Mother

Grandad was the manager of the London Brick Company's tile works near Scalford, Melton Mowbray in Leicestershire. Uncle George was the Chief Engineer and had built a little locomotive and narrow-gauge railway track which ran all round the extensive brick yard, across the road, and down to the railway sidings. All this was my playground. I watched every process of the tile making from the digging of the clay through the shaping, drying, kilning and helped to stack the little wagons ready to be linked up to the loco' and taken down the sidings. Each midday, I sat up beside 'Lod', the lame driver, hopping down to open gates, and change the track points over when necessary as we thundered across the road and down to the loading bay in time to see the powerful, reliable goods train come slowly into sight in a cloud of black smoke and hissing steam as it emerged from under the bridge and come to a halt in a scream of grinding metal.

How I loved being taken across the track and lifted in with the driver and fireman to be allowed to blow the whistle and pull on the brakes while the empty wagons were shunted off and the full ones hooked on. I was enjoying what small boys dream of and no-one cared how dirty I got or worried where I was - at least I had some shorts by then, and I wanted to be a train driver when I grew up, not a steam-roller driver any more… that was last year's ambition!

When it rained, I was allowed to amuse myself in the Dickensian office where uncle Fred and Grandad usually were. Sitting on a high stool at a sloping desk I wrote letters home, then play on the typewriter until I'd jammed the keys up, but I was more tolerated there than in the house with Grandma. *Lionville House* and *Lionville Cottages* were all part of the Brick company. Plumbing was still very basic, the only toilet being in an adjacent out-house, but modern compared to ours. This was the *Elsan* – a large tin can containing some evil smelling, tar-like chemical called *Jeyes fluid*. The can had a proper seat with lid and was emptied over a bank in the next field once a week and was thought to be hygienic! The grass was very green! Grandma thought herself posh as she bought the boxed sheets of *Jeyes* tissues which were considerably kinder on the anatomy than the Farmer's almanac. The house itself was considered modern because Uncle George had installed electricity. This was produced by some mysterious (to me) method involving a row of glass jars (Leclanché Cells) containing acid, which stood on a shelf in the under-stairs cupboard, and on no account must be touched! When Grandma wanted to iron she wound the handle on the internal telephone and asked Uncle George for "more juice please!" and he ran the generator in the engine shed at the yard for her. He lived at the first cottage with Aunty Muriel and had a great love of racing motorbikes and *Morgan* cars, while Uncle Fred, then in his early twenties, favoured a two-seater Singer convertible and lots of girlfriends. I had to sit on the current 'auntie's' knee when we went out.

The six weeks school holiday passed quickly and I was brought back again in time for school. The maid, Kitty, had left to go and work at the Hall School for more money and had been replaced by a 'Mary'. She was passable, not as kindly as Kitty, and was a bit slow and lumbering, lazy.

She also had to wear the brown dress with lace collar and frilly apron in the afternoons - a sign of the gracious middle-class living that mother tried to emulate -

DEAR MUMMY & DADDY,

Uncle George and auntie Muriel came
back yesterday and brought me
a fountain pen; which I am writing
with.

Grandad took me to Donnington on
Sunday, with Grandma and aunt Alice
from Leicester, and while we were
there Roger came in Mr. Gray's car, and
we had a picnic.

+ + + + + + + + + + +
+ + + + + + Love from Monica + +

+ + +

In case you
don't know this is
a small "g".

Monica says she
always send you nice
post cards & you always
Hy send her comics

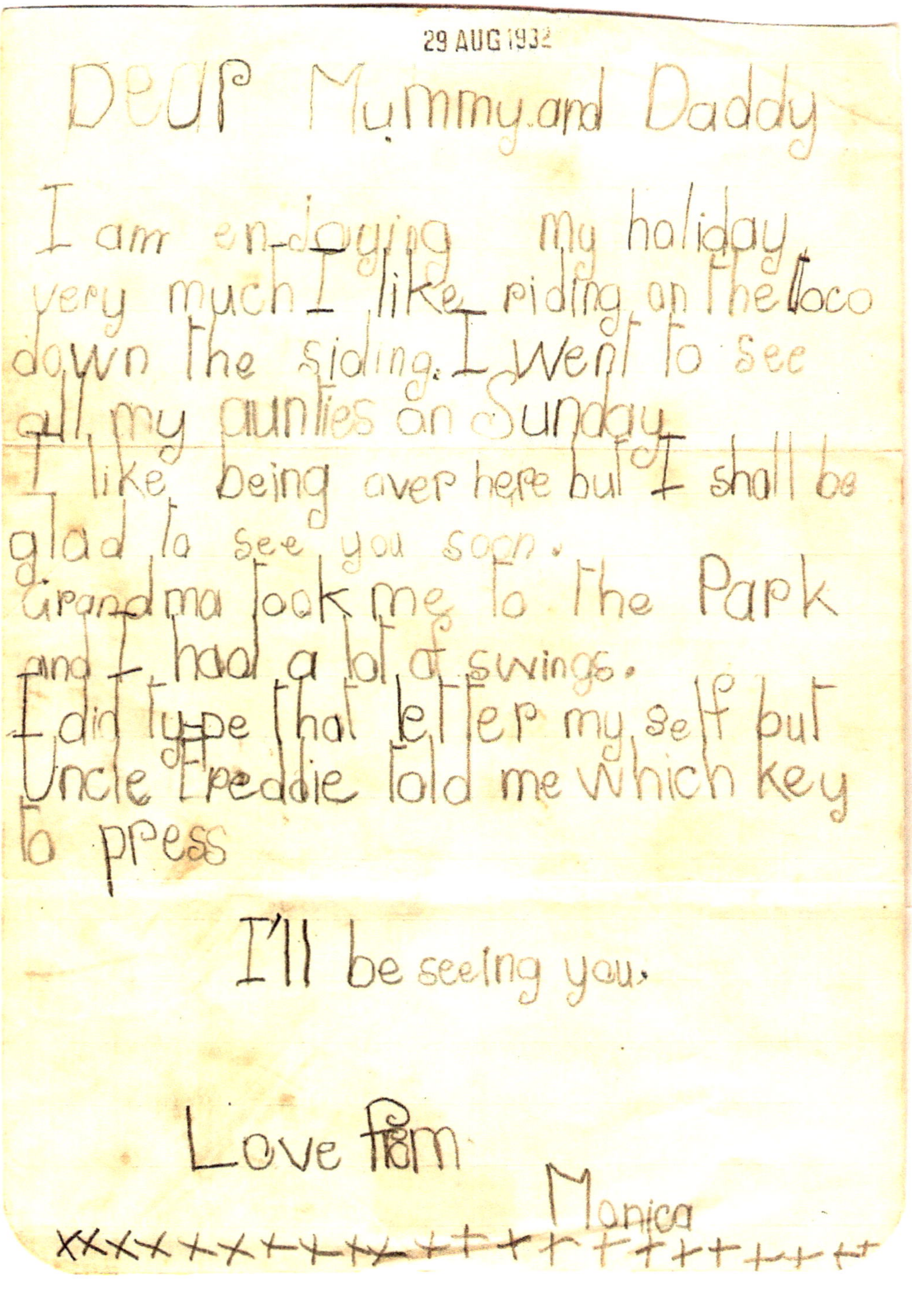

29 AUG 1932

Dear Mummy and Daddy

I am en-joying my holiday
very much I like riding on the loco
down the siding. I went to see
all my aunties on Sunday
I like being over here but I shall be
glad to see you soon.
Grandma took me to the Park
and I had a lot of swings.
I did type that letter myself but
Uncle Freddie told me which key
to press

I'll be seeing you.

Love from

Monica

xxxxxxxxxxxxxxxxxxxxxxxxx

wrote on thursday

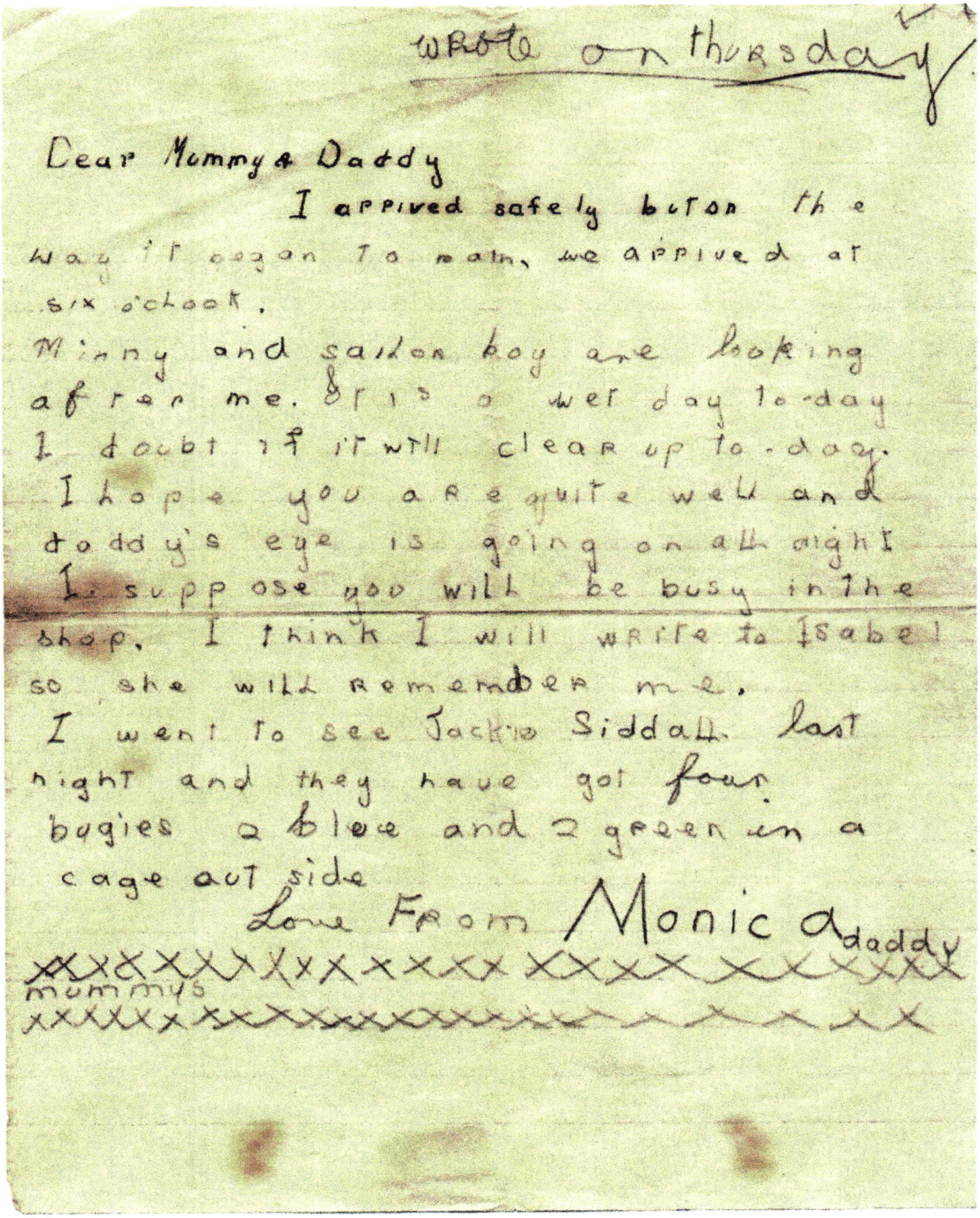

Dear Mummy & Daddy
I arrived safely but on the way it began to rain, we arrived at six o'clock.
Minny and sailor boy are looking after me. It is a wet day to-day I doubt if it will clear up to-day.
I hope you are quite well and daddy's eye is going on all right
I suppose you will be busy in the shop. I think I will write to Isabel so she will remember me.
I went to see Jackie Siddall last night and they have got four bugies 2 blue and 2 green in a cage out side
Love From Monica
XXXXXXXXXXXXXXXXXXXXXXXXX daddy
mummys
XXXXXXXXXXXXXXXXXXXXXXXXXXX

nevertheless, I was still threatened with the workhouse if I scuffed my shoes.

That frightened me, lots of things frightened me, especially at night in bed. There was the ivy that tapped ghostly messages on the old sash windows as they rattled with the wind. Owls in the woods across the road, hooted and screeched, followed by blood-curdling squawks and hissing during a territorial dispute of the neighbour's cats. Blocking my ears from the sounds I could then see the pattern on the wallpaper moving, forming such hideous shapes and faces. Shut my eyes and I could still  hear clock ticking, playing tricks, fast, slow loud and soft as if talking, then the ivy, - another owl – "MUM–MEE!!- "get to sleep, you naughty girl!" many nights I suffered with pains in my calves - leg ache referred to as growing pains by the grown-ups. That didn't get much sympathy either! The worst fear was a thunderstorm. If you lie with your head right down at the bottom of the bed even with your eyes shut you can still see and feel the lightning, and you can't breathe either.

At eight years old I was enrolled as a brownie into the 'Fairies' six. If I had known about those thick brown woollen stockings, which were uncomfortably attached on lengths of elastic to buttons on my liberty Bodice, I could have voiced some objections beforehand, but I had no choice – I was drafted in because it was the 'in thing'. The only way I could show displeasure of stockings was to over-exaggerate the robotic walk they caused – like a puppet with elastic strings. Mother was not amused.- And why did we have to dance around a stuffed furry owl which sat on an outsize toadstool while we sang to it?!

Silver Jubilee 1935 - George V and Queen Mary

The whole village celebrated this with a procession of carts, lorries and anything that could move. For days everyone had been making red, white and blue rosettes and streamers from crêpe paper. The houses, shops, railings and lampposts were festooned and flags flying. Our hands, faces and clothes were stained by sticky damp-fingered handling of this paper, fortunately the day dawned dry and sunny or the effects could have been disastrous. We brownies, overwhelmed by large rosettes sewn to our woolly hats, were crammed on a bunting-draped lorry studded with even more rosettes, to tirelessly wave our little paper flags as the lorry crawled its way behind the other four similarly bedecked lorries, two tractors, the coal cart scrubbed for the occasion, Jot's brown van and a few shire horses - truly, a grand procession!

It came to a halt at the village hall where everyone went in for tea. Lengths of trestle-tables were disguised by yet more red, white and blue crêpe paper and rosettes. Party food was not sophisticated in 1935, just plates piled high with curled up, hand cut, white bread sandwiches, filled, or rather scraped, with *Shippam's Paste* – pilchard, anchovy or salmon flavoured, and perhaps a few Potted meat ones. Then, came the jelly and blancmange, over spilling the dishes onto the red, white and blue paper which stained our fingers and daubed our faces. Lastly came the plates of buns, iced, currant, chocolate and bright pink, all made and served by the worthy village ladies in their floral pinafores. To drink, there was tea, a tepid, milky, oversweet strong brew poured from a battered aluminium, gallon teapot, that was so unwieldy that aiming for the cup was largely guesswork and added to the unsavoury mess already on the patriotic table décor. All children were presented with a commemorative jubilee mug, and another one at school, and yet another from the county. – If we had taken more care of them, they may now be valuable.

Scrubbing floors and eating dry bread in the work house was still a constant threat to me if I wore a hole in my sock or shoes and frightened me into trying to walk around puddles and not kick stones. There were other threats too to reckon with such as not to tell fibs because "Be sure the Devil will find you out" – whatever that meant, and you must not do anything sneaky or unkind as "God will know and punish you" – That makes sure that you can't even pick your nose without worrying, so I grew an outsized conscience which, according to mother, is the thing that sits on your shoulder telling you to do good things and not listen to the Devil which sits on the other shoulder telling you to do bad things. This caused much conflict trying to explain a torn dress or why I was late for tea. How petty it all seems now.

The Tailor

We could not have been as hard up as they would have me believe, as twice a year the tailor came to the house. Other village children seemed to have much prettier and more interesting clothes than I did. There was Eileen's red coat with a rabbit fur collar, Agnes's white ankle socks and black patent ankle-strap shoes, but these were considered 'common' by my  mother, so we had a tailor from Scarborough! Mr Story was another Dickensian character, with a starched wing collar, heavy worsted suit with his gold watch-chain dangling from the waistcoat pocket. His long shiny chin and face were topped off with an even shinier bald head which gave him the appearance of an oversized leprechaun with spectacles.

On the first visit he brought books of samples of suitings, worsteds and Harris tweeds which were argued over for two weeks. Choosing a style was easier, there only were three to choose from. Father and mother were measured, and then me for a dreaded coat and perhaps a pleated tunic with plenty of room for growth!

I particularly remember a cream and brown, small checked, Harris tweed coat, shapeless, heavy, long, miles too big, with a half belt at the back. Haute couture it was not! "Very classical and in very good taste" I was told. I hated it! Every opportunity was taken to jump on it and kick it around the bedroom in the hope of wearing it out, but it was made of iron and resisted every form of ill – treatment, It wouldn't even look dirty, and I never did grow into it! Marks and Spencer's was unknown to us then, mother made all my dresses, in the same style, from shantung, a natural, cream coloured, raw silk - sometimes it had green spots on. Cardigans and jumpers were hand-knitted with matching berets – quite awful! But the worst of all were the knitted bathing suits – a pink one and a blue one. Both were big, but tolerable when dry, but as soon as they got wet the weight of the water dragged them down to the knees! This, I felt, was very demoralising and was delighted when the pink one shrank in the wash and turned into a stable but stiff, shapeless piece of pale pink felt. It was quite uncomfortable, but to my mind, much more in vogue. Thus the blue one was left for moths to enjoy as no-one dare wash it.

Health

All school children got mumps, measles and chicken pox in their season as we only had a vaccination for small pox. I got whooping cough too, followed by frequent bouts of bronchitis. The treatment meant long days of boredom in bed, breathing in pungent fumes of 'Friar's balsam' that was kept boiling in an old pan on the top of a Valor paraffin stove. As darkness came, the cut-out designs on the stove flickered eerie patterns on the walls and ceiling. Twice a day my back and chest were rubbed with warm camphorated oil and covered with warm flanelette, and all I could remember eating was 'Pobs' - a basin full of white bread covered with hot milk sugar and butter. Very nourishing, I was told. Then came the building up process with a parent on each side coaxing, pleading and threatening. They shovelled in Parishes food', (a foul tasting iron tonic which turned teeth black) 'California Syrup of figs', for the bowels, whether you needed it or not, and, if I hadn't already thrown up, a spoonful of codliver oil to top it off. Sometimes they mixed all three together because it would taste nicer! Thank goodness we now have antibiotics

To guard against colds and flu in winter, we wore a little drawstring bag around our necks containing a lump of camphor it also kept the moths away. Mother sewed a few wads of orange, impregnated cotton wool called *Thermogene* onto her vest!

 A new invention called an 'Iodine Locket' then superseded the camphor bag. Most of the kids wore this double metal disc on a string, which exuded Iodine fumes instead, - very smart!

In spring everyone seemed to get 'Heat Spots', very itchy, and due to the overheating of the blood in the  springtime - so the old wives said! To combat this, you were dosed with large, bright yellow sulphur tablets which gave you the runs, thus "cooling the blood".

 By autumn I was being got at with Cod liver oil and malt to get me fit to resist the winter ailments. You either love it or hate it and with the scent of the raw cod liver oil still in my nostrils, I hated it! Capsules were not invented then.

No amount of cajoling, forcing, nose-holding or threats could get this claggy, nauseous concoction past my lips and I put up a good fight. One thing I gave my parents credit for --- they resorted to bribery! For one month, without missing a day, I voluntarily heaved, gulped and retched my way to winning a *Mamod* microscope! Never again could I face another spoonful. The microscope opened up a whole new fascinating insight into spiders legs, flies wings, ribbon, hair and blood. I was never offered bribery again or the price might have been very much higher.

Filey 1935

When I was almost nine years old, we moved to Filey. Number two Union Street had a large shop with a fitting room and stockroom, three bedrooms and large sitting room, a real bathroom, and separate flush toilet on the first floor and three more attic bedrooms and a box-room on the second floor. Downstairs was a comfortable living/dining room with a modern Yorkist range - enamelled, (no more black leading!) a good sized kitchen, pantry and conservatory. A narrow path led from a small yard to a tiny garden and brick outhouse which held the coalhouse, another toilet and father's workshop. We really did seem to be going up in the world especially now we had a maid who 'lived in'. Another Mary who slept up in the attic, had bad teeth, bad breath and was quite ugly, she came from Durham.

Changing to the Council school was no problem, the only noticeable difference was that most of the boys smelt of fish instead of manure and had a playground to themselves.

My father now decided to coach me in arithmetic and English because it was his wish for me to win a scholarship to the girls' high school in Bridlington. Many miserable hours were spent as he tried to instil the delights of fractions and decimals while my friends played outside. Wandering thoughts were brought back to reality by a sharp cuff across the ear, only once, but it was the expletive "Duck egg!" that hurt the most, it was the only time he sounded really cross with me and that was worst insult he was capable off. Sadly, he began to be ill more frequently, and I saw him collapse on the hearthrug with blood coming out of his mouth from the damaged lungs.

I was very frightened. He was taken to a sanatorium for six months and I was not allowed to go and see him, so I still had to spend my summer holidays at the Brickyard.

He wrote lovely long letters to me and knew where all the birds' nests were. For a few weeks he would come home and work again and then have to return to the Isolation Units for pulmonary tuberculosis at Cottingham. If penicillin had been discovered then he would have survived longer.

Mother tried too hard to play the role of father as well and became even stricter than before, giving Mary and I a hard time. Mary had to work very hard to achieve Mother's standards and had very little time off.

She was always sent to bring me home from a party much earlier than any of the other children which was most embarrassing. I was having good fun at the school Christmas party in 1937, we had slipped playing musical mats, cheated at musical parcels, and been pushed over at musical chairs. The salmon paste sandwiches, jelly and buns were eaten and Father Christmas was about to arrive when Mary appeared to take me home, "Oh no, not yet! I'm not ready!" and perhaps I stamped my foot. Outside, she told me the reason, "Your Daddy is dying and wants to see you." In a blinding of hot tears I was rushed home to find a very pale, ailing Father. I had always thought he was old, but at a few days after his 38th birthday his fragile life was ebbing away before I had begun to really know him. I cried for him, I cried for myself and the guilt I felt for not wanting to leave the party and I cried because I was scolded for spoiling the green velvet dress with my tears.

For four nights I listened to the tortured breathing and moans in the next bedroom, willing him to get better. On Christmas morning early, I looked as usual to see if Father Christmas had filled my pillow case – yes he had! By the time I had unwrapped a book and a doll, Mother came in to say that Daddy had died at 4am. It wasn't a happy Christmas. I cried.

The coffin stood open in the bedroom until the time of the funeral. I was told to look in frequently to kiss him and to put in some flowers before the lid was secured. This, I did, in horror of his waxen pallor. But his expression was peaceful though gaunt. They didn't let me go to the funeral and instead I was sent on the bus to Bridlington to spend the day with a step-aunt and cousin Tony. A few days later I saw his ghost walk around to the workshop but didn't tell Mother. I cried.

High School

In May 1937, I sat for the entrance exam for Bridlington high school for girls in hope of a scholarship but only managed to get a free place which meant that the tuition was free, but books, uniform, travel and everything else had to be paid for. This gave rise to a few grumbles from Mother but it did not deter her from buying another silk dress and joining the local golf club.

The list of clothing I required was daunting and could only be purchased from one shop in Bridlington – an expensive one!

1	Dark green worsted tunic with sash.
2	Dark green cotton tunic with sash and matching voluminous 'Walter Raleigh' style knickers.
1	Blazer with broad green, white and black vertical stripes.
1	Gabardine Mackintosh, green with matching hat.
1	Thick wool green winter coat and black velour hat.
3	Silk poplin blouses and tie.
3	Viyella winter blouses.
1 or 2	Pure silk blouses for special days.
2	Summer dresses with the matching 'Walter Raleighs'.
	Panama hat, indoor shoes, plimsolls and lacrosse boots.
3	Pairs each winter stockings and summer stockings.
	Sports pullover, shoe bag and table napkin in a pochette

and the grossest garments of all –

2	Pairs of thick, green down-to-the-knees knickers which couldn't be washed very often as the dye ran and they shrank so they required four pairs of white 'liners' resembling old men's underpants to wear underneath!
	And 1 laboratory overall.

In September, I started the new routine. Getting up at seven am, cooking my own breakfast, walking to the station to catch the 7.50am train for the twelve mile journey to Bridlington which stopped at four stations on the way and arriving back at 4.45pm.

On the train

Travelling to school by steam train was much more interesting than going by bus – there were several distractions to help pass the forty-five minute journey.

First of all were the press-ups. Apart from one carriage which had a short corridor and toilet plus compartments for six people, the rest were single compartments for eight passengers. The girls were allocated two of these and also two for the boys. Above the seats was a luggage rack on each side so the idea is to hold onto the rail on one side and hook your feet over the other side, then count how many press-ups you can do before falling off!

Next came the balancing, all in a row standing up, straddled with one foot on each seat when the train rattled at its fastest between stations. We usually ended up in a heap on a bend!

The feat that now makes me shudder at the thought was to open the door and climb out onto the narrow running board and inch your way along clinging to the door and window frames. The girls in the next compartment hung out of the window to grab you and either opened the door to pull you in or dragged you in through the window – don't even think about it!

On the mornings I left it a bit late, it saved time by roller-skating to the station, a bit later still and I had to skate down the platform with the train just moving off, to be dragged into the carriage by the others whilst 'Fatty' the guard shouted abuse and the station master just stood open-mouthed.

In winter, the snow hung in picturesque undulations over the steep cuttings on the way to Speeton. One morning, some had collapsed and caused a miniature avalanche, blocking the train, Great fun! All the schoolchildren, boys and girls leapt out onto the track and pelted each other and 'Fatty' who was a dejected hunched figure having to walk back to Hunmanby to summon help for the rescue. The long wait for the relief engine to push ours out of the snow made us late for school – Hurrah!

Tourist attractions at Filey

Bonzo the Seal

In a small tin shed, richly stinking of stale fish, and situated on the cobble landing, swam 'Bonzo', in a too small galvanised water tank.

He had scars on his nose, head and back, ragged flippers and pungent halitosis. Fishermen had rescued him from the beach after a storm and thought they could 'make a bob or two' by charging one penny each to see him and feed him with a herring while wetting you through trying to turn round in the tank and snorting. He eventually died of old age, and probably boredom.

The Pierrots

In the 30's, most seaside resorts had a beach concert party performing twice a day in the summer season on the sand, and on the grass at high tide., pushing their piano and dragging their tatty basket of props. They were really quite scruffy, Gus the small one, was the ugliest man I have ever seen and the 'lady' had big hairy arms, – I thought they were wonderful – but corny!

Modern Surgery

One day, on rising and contemplating the possibilities of a summer Saturday morning, mother shouted casually and almost sweetly "don't bother getting dressed this morning, and, by the way you can't have breakfast either - you're having your tonsils out at ten o'clock!" I was slightly miffed at not being warned earlier, why the secret? I was eleven years old!

Filey only had two doctors, and they both arrived with their bags at 9:45 am. Then I was ushered into the upstairs sitting-room, shocked at its transformation. The settee and chairs were covered with white sheets as when spring cleaning, there was a single bed in the corner, and the dining table in the square bay – windows had been covered with blankets with a white sheet over it that was to be the operating table! Being too frightened to make any protest, I climbed up, as instructed, and lay down in terror, looking up into two pairs of hairy nostrils. Down over my mouth and nose came the gauze-covered metal mask, then the instructions to breathe deeply and count as the doctor dripped chloroform onto the mask (the rag and bottle method!) I remember counting to five whilst struggling violently because I couldn't breathe, and strong hands holding me down before being spun into thankful oblivion. On waking, back in bed, my throat felt full of broken glass and I immediately relieved my stomach of all the blood I had swallowed, causing my mother to come running, but too late to save herself a pile of laundry. On the third day in bed without food and little to drink, I was coaxed to try and swallow strawberries and ice-cream – a very painful 'reward'. Thankfully, the treatment these days, is not so barbaric and inconsiderate.

At War

In September 1939, war was declared against Germany and everyone was in fear that we were going to be bombed or shot at in the next few days, but life went on as normal for several months, except for the preparations and apprehension.

Mary left to get higher wages elsewhere, so I had to learn to wash my own neck and hair! The rationing of butter, meat, cheese, bread, soap, clothes and even sweets, was introduced by means of cards and coupons. In a small town like Filey, no one went short of anything. Shop keepers bartered coupons amongst themselves, and mother bartered shoe coupons for fish, crabs and bread. She refused rabbits and mackerel, claiming that they were vermin! The beach and cliffs were closed off with barbed wire, leaving only a few yards open, as access for the fishing boats and swimming. The hotels and some boarding houses were taken over by Royal Engineers, Durham light infantry and other armed forces. A favourite field near the station was made into a parade ground for the soldiers and is now the bus station.

All homes and premises had to have blackout curtains or boards, keeping the women folk busy sewing yards of black sateen for every window and outer door. Street lights were painted black, cutting visibility down to a minimum. Cars, bicycle lamps and torches had to have black cardboard in, with just a small slot allowing only a small glimmer of light through. Later when the bombing did start it just caused a bit of a stir when the air raid wardens tapped on your door and shouted "Put that light out!" if the tiniest chink of light was showing - "and tell Monica to stop reading!"

Equipment to be caried by all fire watchers

1. Belt to go around the waist with ten hooks to support six full sand bags and four buckets of water
2. Axe in belt.
3. 1 Stirrup pump to be carried over left shoulder.
4. 1 Extending ladder on the right shoulder.
5. 1 Whistle to be carried in the mouth.
6. 1 Long handled shovel to be tucked under the left arm.
7. 2 Wet blankets to be carried on the head.
8. 1 Steel helmet with turn-up brim to carry spare water.
9. Spare sand to be carried in all pockets.
10. 1 box of matches to light incendiary bombs which fail to explode.

BY ORDER

Grocery Prices

Item	1933	1938	1941-43
Beef Ribs (lb)	1s 2d	1s 2 ½d	1s 6d
Mutton Leg (lb)	1s 2 ¼d	1s 3 ¾d	1s 4d
Pork (lb)	10d	10d	1s 0d
Bacon (lb)	11d	1s 3 ½d	1s 5d
Bread (4lb)	7 ½d	9d	10d
Butter (lb)	1s 2 ¼d	1s 4 ½d	1s 2 ½d
Sugar (lb)	2 ½d	2 ½d	3d
Eggs (per doz)	1s 6d	1s 6d	2s 0d
Potatoes (7lb)	5 ½d	6 ¼d	1s 2d
Cheese (lb)	9 ½d	10 ½d	1s 1d
Tea (lb)	1s 9 ½d	2s 3 ½d	2s 1d

Filey Girl Guides cutting strips for camoflage nets. 1940

Camoflaging gun emplacements with branches

War Work

Most girls of my age were in the Girl Guides at that time, and we had great fun working to clock up the hundred hours of service needed to achieve our National Service badge.

There was a desperate need for metal to make ammunitions so the iron railings round the front of houses had to be sawn off and collected to help the War Effort - We pushed an old handcart around the streets collecting old pans, kettles, bathtubs and any old scrap metal we could cadge – just like *Steptoe*. It kept us usefully occupied and well entertained especially when overloaded, wobbly wheels and an enamel chamber pot rolls down the road.

Gun emplacements were built on the cliffs which needed camouflage. We cut up short strips of sack-cloth to tie onto the large nets which covered the anti-aircraft guns, then collected branches of leaves to disguise the concrete 'Pill boxes' - all good fun!

First Aid course became a must for the locals, but we were still too young to join the St John's Ambulance courses. This was overcome by offering ourselves as 'patients', thus earning more National Service hours for the badge. Three evenings a week we listened to a very worthy Mr. Cockerill expounding on "Injuries to the *harm*, *foreharm*, and the '*and*" as we were bandaged, splinted and stretchered.

War, so far, had been carefree and amusing until bombing became more frequent and many nights were disturbed by the wailing siren, distant explosions of the bombs and landmines, and the anti-aircraft guns on the cliffs. Flamborough Head was a landmark for the German raiders heading for Leeds, Sheffield and Hull. On the their return, bombs would be off-loaded, many landing in the bay and only three fell on the top of Filey Brigg - you can still see the holes.

The Sea Scouts became voluntary Fire Watchers and learnt how to put out incendiary bombs with buckets of water and stirrup-pumps. Mother did a twice-weekly air raid duty, manning the telephones which received the warnings of approaching aircraft before the sirens sounded, she also helped at the forces N.A.A.F.I. canteen making mountains of sandwiches – cold baked beans mashed with a token sprinkle of grated cheese!! Everyone did their bit, and morale and humour ran high.

In 1940, Air Raid shelters were being built, large concrete communal ones for

FILEY GIRL GUIDES' HELPING HAND

Filey Girl Guides give a helping hand to evacuees yesterday.
—[N.E.]

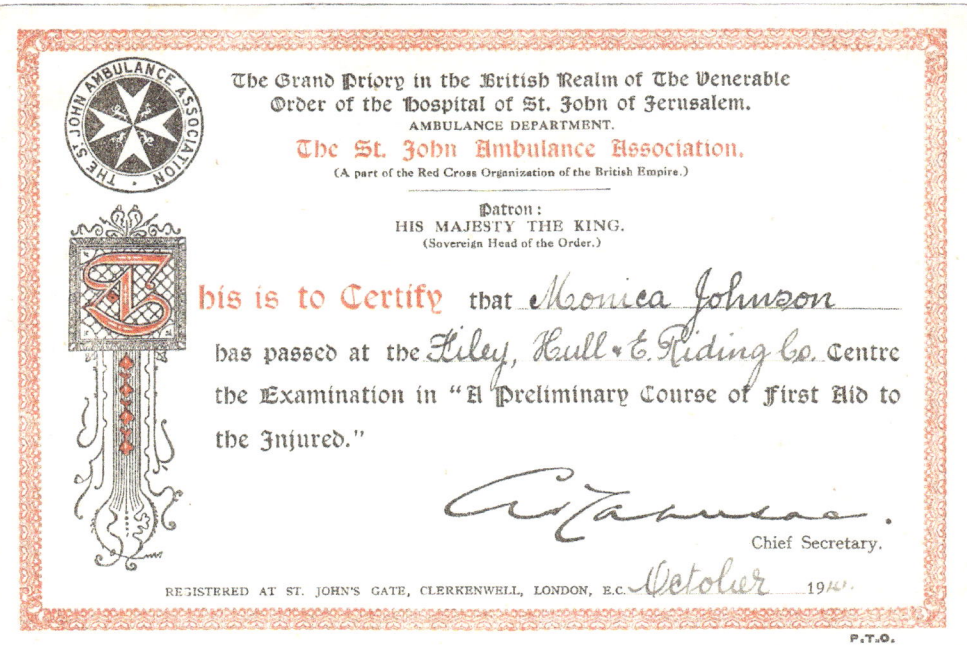

The Grand Priory in the British Realm of The Venerable
Order of the Hospital of St. John of Jerusalem.

AMBULANCE DEPARTMENT.

The St. John Ambulance Association.

(A part of the Red Cross Organization of the British Empire.)

Patron:
HIS MAJESTY THE KING.
(Sovereign Head of the Order.)

This is to Certify that *Monica Johnson*

has passed at the *Filey, Hull & E. Riding Co.* Centre
the Examination in "A Preliminary Course of First Aid to
the Injured."

Chief Secretary.

REGISTERED AT ST. JOHN'S GATE, CLERKENWELL, LONDON, E.C. *October* 19..

P.T.O.

perhaps thirty people off the streets, and if you had a garden large enough to excavate a large hole, you had an 'Anderson' shelter topped with corrugated iron, sandbags, turf – very muddy and damp inside. Ours was a 'Morrison', a steel table shelter, about five foot six inches square, which sat in the middle of the living room instead of the dining table. The sides were of re-enforced wire mesh and made you feel like a caged animal when trying to sleep on the hard make-shift bed inside, where you took refuge when the siren sounded. It wasn't much use as a table either!

Many children were being evacuated. I had a medical check and had been booked in to sail to Canada on the ship 'City of Benares' and was to live with a great Aunt Cita on a farm in Saskatchewan. Although I'd never heard of her until then, it sounded like an adventure. So I didn't fuss. The Germans started to bomb evacuaee boats so mother changed her mind and I stayed at home. The 'City of Benares', full of children, was sunk.

Evacuees from the towns began to arrive into Filey by the trainload and the Girl Guides were given the task of meeting them and herding the bewildered, pale and tearstained children into some kind of order and leading them from the station down to the Infants school. We carried as many of their cases as possible, but most of them were quite poor and brought very little with them, if anything, except their gasmask and large identity label tied with string to a buttonhole. When the weary, pathetic little procession arrived at the school there was a drink, a biscuit and a paper bag of provisions for each one, then we delivered them to their homes where, I am sure, they were put straight into the bath!

In October, 1940 Grandfather Palmer died, and Grandma had a stroke and came to live with us, which stressed mother even more, which I suppose is understandable now, but at that time seemed a constant clash between three strong-willed females – not a happy situation!

Sent Away

Autumn 1940

Whether it was for my safety or mother's comfort, I'm not sure. Without warning I was packed off to Bridlington to be a 'Weekly Boarder' in a seafront, small hotel taken over by the school. There, we slid down the bannisters, gargled the national anthem with pink Glycothymol every night at bedtime, and spent many hours through the night air raids lying on the lounge floor playing 'Pick-up-sticks' and 'Happy families'. It was quite a happy atmosphere, but just so embarrassing every morning when we had to walk more than a mile in an orderly crocodile. As we came to the railway bridge, the Filey train was nearly always passing over with all my mates hanging out of the windows waving and jeering! I stayed for two terms.

Summer 1941

Because I was still forbidden to speak to boys, and because I couldn't see what the reason was, we all chattered our way down from the station and stood at the corner for a few minutes before going home. There was always one well-meaning gossip who had already called in at the shop just to say – "I've just seen your Monica at the corner – talking to the boys!" They never mentioned the girls there too, so by the time I walked through the door with a cheery "Hello" I met with a blast of maternal fury and told I was getting "out of hand!" That was how I came to be packed off Foston Hall, near York, for two weeks in the summer holidays. This pleasant old country house had been taken over by the school for the boarders, who had now been evacuated from Bridlington, and so was being used to help with funding during the school holidys.

We were taken to the Castle museums at York, then quite new, and owned by the grandfather of a pupil, thus giving us free admission. Enforced painting classes took us into fields of sheep and the grounds of Castle Howard. The kitchen gardens gave us ample fruit and stomach ache while helping with chores, before sliding down the bannisters and gargling.

Sledging down church ravine – 1940
Note – "Pixie Hats" worn by most girls.
These were made from a scarf folded in half and stitched
about six inches from centre fold. The boys wore knitted balaclava helmets.

Dormitory 5 at Foston Hall.

View of Donkey Hill. Foston Hall 1941.

Making the best of it

The latest craze became Plane Spotting; you bought a book of pictures and silhouettes of English and German aeroplanes and ticked them off as you saw them. Convoys of cargo boats regularly passed northwards off Flamborough Head, flanked by Destroyers and corvettes of the Royal Navy, and Barrage Balloons. To sit on the cliffs or foreshore with our books, watch the aerial dog-fights and see guns spitting streams of tracer bullets from the pill boxes was a good afternoon's entertainment with much jeering and cheering.

As the war heated up in 1941, trains were being bombed We could hear they were quite close and our teachers struggled to keep our attention down in the cellar at school as the crumbling plaster fell on to our books with each loud bang. After school, down at the station, it was an amusing diversion to be taken by bus to Flamborough station, then by train to Hunmanby where we climbed into the back of an army vehicle, the business men too, for the last few miles to Filey. Although a large stretch of track had been destroyed, and the afternoon train machine-gunned, we were never afraid, it just seemed exciting. For a few days, until the track was repaired, we had to suffer the jeers of the school bus children. There followed days, when, to our joy, the train was late and lessons were missed and disrupted.

As thoughtless teenagers it seldom crossed our minds that while so many people were being killed, injured and risking their lives, we were enjoying all the gory details, and diversions such as looking for shrapnel and aeroplane bits after an air crash and bragging about who was nearest the last raid.

One night, the sirens had fetched us out of bed for the third time, I looked out of the window at the searchlights and was listening to the guns when I saw lots of 'things' falling down. These were some of the two thousand incendiary bombs that fell on Filey that night. Within minutes the town was engulfed in an orange glow. The laundry burnt down and several houses were hit, but many fell in gardens and were soon extinguished by the owners or the boys with stirrup pumps. No-one was hurt and it caused much gossip the next day.

My pocket money increased from sixpence (2½ old pence) to one shilling (5p) which bought me a comic, some sweets and a ticket to the cinema on Saturday afternoons. For this I had to polish the downstairs brasses - ie. a two inch wide strip surrounding the door-mat well, four other strips between the front door and inner door, six fancy door knobs, the letter box and a wide collar around the door bell!

1941

A new organisation formed - the Women's Junior Air Corps. (W.J.A.C) which I joined with a few of my cronies, the boys joined a similar group. The uniform was much smarter than the guides and we really thought ourselves 'cool' in grey skirts, bright blue shirts, tie and dashing grey 'Glengarry' airman's cap. Many hours were spent marching and being drilled on the Army Parade Ground to perfect our, right wheel, left wheel, form fours, slow march and quick march and so be smarter than the boys when we carried the flags to church once a month on Sundays. With two friends, I went to church every Sunday, perhaps for a few wrong reasons, i.e. - escaping from mother and grandma, being able to talk to the choirboys afterwards and walking slowly back home by way of the cliffs and the promenade. I was usually in trouble for being late for lunch. But I grew to enjoy the services and atmosphere of the lovely old, twelfth century, S.t Oswald's church. Every week during the war we belted out Hymn 370 "Eternal Father strong to save".

"Oh hear us when we cry to thee,
for those in peril on the sea".

Oct. 1942

My pocket money had risen dramatically to two shillings (12½ p) and sixpence but I had to do more chores and was expected to put some in the bank also. The war continued and there was a fear that harmful gases would soon be used, so we had to learn the differences between them. Mustard gas would burn the skin, tear gas smelt of pear drops and made the eyes stream, and chorine gas damaged the lungs. As an experiment, a large air raid, shelter was converted to have sealed doors, and groups of people went in and walked around in circles wearing gas masks whilst some tear gas was released. We all looked very weird, giving me the giggles, and it is not easy laughing in a gasmask, it makes disgusting noises and you laugh even more, till it hurts. We waved our handkerchiefs about hoping to catch some gas so we could bring them out later to see if it made us cry! It didn't but everyone got a little certificate for attending.

1942 School

Without working too hard, I managed to keep up with most subjects (except history - 3%), homework mostly being done on the morning train, kneeling on the filthy floor and writing essays with books resting on seats. A jolting train does not enhance the neatness of work. In winter, in all weathers, we had to play hockey, lacrosse and netball. Summer time was for cricket, rounders and tennis. Tennis practice I found boring, so a few of us found refuge over a wall into the graveyard near an apple tree.

Also this summer we took the school certificate exams, now called "O" levels. I was fifteen and passed in seven subjects, but had disappointed everyone by not getting higher grades and 'Matriculating'.

The long summer holidays were now spent in Filey, barefooted, swimming and climbing the rocks on Filey Brigg where I was forbidden to go because it was dangerous, in fact most things I wanted to do were forbidden – Teenagers might recognise that phase.

Since grandma came to live with us there was always an uneasy atmosphere, if mother wasn't shouting at me, she was shouting at grandma for losing her glasses or some trivial deed, so we tried to keep out of the way of each other. Strangely, grandma always loomed into sight with her walking stick when I was somewhere I shouldn't be, like the Amusement arcade on the cobble landing or jumping off the promenade onto a sandcastle with a gang of boys and girls, - mother knew all about it before I got home. Trouble again – "thanks grandma!" – In later years I grew very fond of her, she had great fortitude and I wish I had talked to her more often.

6th Form Autumn term 1942

Our classroom was in the old house wing, it was elegant, with an oak floor, marble fire place, beamed ceiling, 'po faced' portraits of past benefactors on the wall and a black bearskin rug. Six of us shared a large table in a very relaxed happy atmosphere which should have encouraged work, having only four subjects to concentrate on - Art, French, Biology and Commercial studies. Slowly it was dawning on me that one day I would have to work and earn my own living. Having grown out of the train driver and steam roller driver phase, I started to wonder what would be the easiest option. Perhaps a bank, - two doors from home and they only work from 10am until 3pm, - So I thought! That could be boring, stuck at a desk, how about teaching? - They only work from 9am - 4pm and have lots of holidays!! That's it, I'll teach Art and Biology

It soon became clear that I was certainly not cut out for an office. Book keeping was easy, Shorthand was tedious and I had no aptitude whatever for typing. Scratchy little gramophone records plink-plonked a mindless tune intended to keep us in rhythm with pressing the typewriter keys, no good, I got the giggles!

If I concentrated on what I was supposed to write, I was too slow and out of time with the plink-plonk, so was spotted by the sad-faced old school secretary trying to teach us. To keep in time with everyone else and avoid reprimand, I found it impossible to type the given exercise, thus making no further progress than page after page in every lesson of 'ASDFG and QWERTY.' In perfect time with the music!

My first dance

It was agreed that the boys in the A.T.C (Air Training Corps) and the girls in the W.J.A.C (Women's Junior Air Corps) would get together to organise a dance to raise funds for some current worthy cause. Trying to find a suitable, and cheap hall to hold it in was not easy. The hotels were occupied by military personnel, the tennis pavilion was too expensive and church halls were permanently booked. One of our girls lived at the 'Foords Hotel', the oldest pub in town down Queen Street which had several outbuildings on its premises, including the rifle club and two or three disused houses. One of these was the 'Haunted House', which had a genuine 'priest hole' behind the fire place and stories of smugglers and intrigue. Most of us had explored it at some time hoping to encounter the ghost. Another building was a largish wooden shack, a one-time summer house or holiday cottage which now lent itself to the occasional jumble sale presided over by the W.V.S. ladies - and we could have this free!

Its rough boarded floors were swept, and a host of spiders made homeless with the dusting of a decade of cobweb tangle. A few flags, streamers and balloons festooned from the beams, transformed it sufficiently to be considered suitable, or at least passable!

Prices, tickets and light refreshments were arranged, ie. tea and lemonade! A 'live' band was located, the usual drums, saxophone and piano-accordion were the accepted 'one-up' from a wind-up gramophone, so we were ready and eager for the big night!

There was still one obstacle left for me, during all the activity, I had not yet mentioned it, nor plucked up courage to ask my mother if I could go to this social extravaganza.

As casually as possible, I finally broached the question of attending this dance… "It's for a very good cause!"… silence - then "Mmmm-mm, Well perhaps." - what a relief, but my pleasure was short lived as she added the compromise… "But I shall go too"!! Useless were the protests that no-one else's parents would be there, or that I could be trusted to behave perfectly well on my own.

So, instead of looking forward to having fun with friends, I was dreading the embarrassment of her presence - and not without reason.

"Who's that boy? Not very tidy, is he?", "Who was that boy you've just danced with? He didn't ask you properly, nor did he bring you back to your seat!" *Probably because he was scared of you,* I thought! "Those girls look rather common, I hope they're not friends of yours!" Well, I wouldn't admit it even if they were! I do wish she would keep quiet and let me mix and enjoy myself like everyone else, I can't help it if the boys are wearing hob-nailed boots - there is a war on! Another two hours of agony-spiked pleasure before the musical trio vented their lack of talent into the last walz - ♪♫ "Who's taking ♫ you home ♫ tonight?" ♪♫ I certainly knew 'who' and it wasn't going to be my friend Charles!

That's the last time I shall ask to go to the dance!

A grand day out

One crystal October day, as the train passed by Flamborough Head, the glint of the sun on white cliffs against the blue brilliance of the sea seemed to put a spell on me - and I hadn't done my French homework! We hadn't planned to play truant, Marjory and I; it started as a windup to a very prissy classmate, we just intended to take a different route to school, but the magic of the day took over. Leaving our satchels in the left luggage office we boarded a bus back to Flamborough Head and walked round to North Landing over the cliff path breathing in the beauty. After a swim in the icy water and drying on a handkerchief, we explored the caves, lunched on lemonade and chocolate and caught the bus back in time to catch the train home. A wonderful day out, we thought!

Whilst waiting on the station platform for the other children, there was this feeling all was not well, otherwise, why were they walking down the road, two by two in a very prim orderly crocodile headed by one of the most formidable mistresses? Hiding behind some crates, we watched the train come in, the children being supervised into the carriages and the train pull out without us having a chance to run across to it. "Now, what do we do??" it would be dark soon, and the next train was not for two and a half hours. We had no telephone, but Marjory's Father was a warrant officer in the R.A.F. based in Filey - "So… if I ring daddy and say we've missed the train and won't be home until 6:30pm my little brother can run and tell your mum!" – Good thinking Marjory! She was the one with the money and knew how to make a call from a call box, but she got no further than a sweet "Hello daddy-" when we were pounced on by two burly R.A.F. special police. "Got you! We've been all day looking for you two!" It transpired, that our prim little 'friend' on being asked where Monica and Marjory were, instead of saying what she thought we had done, i.e play truant, she thought she was being tactful and said "I don't know, they were behind us when we got off the train" This, in wartime, in an all-girls school caused a major furore.

The headmistress rang the hospitals, the boys school, to see if any boys were also missing, Marjory's father, and the Police, who also had to call and inform mother. While the big search for two missing school girls had been occupying the whole of Bridlington we had only been aware of having a grand day out, but we paid for it. In deep disgrace we were taken home in the R.A.F. police van straight to Marjory's father to be spanked hard at mother's instruction. He was rather a softie and didn't hurt us too much. It was the good lecture he gave us afterwards about "thinking before acting foolishly", the disregard we'd had for all the trouble we had caused, and the dangers that could have befallen us, that made us feel very contrite and ashamed, but it was still a good day out that I shall always remember. But that was not yet the end of the matter, I was the elder and got the blame!

Flamborough Head

For three weeks I was suspended from school, made to do all the worst household chores, and not allowed out the house, having just missed expulsion by the kind intervention of the vicar and another older friend. Mother only spoke to me in snaps and snarls and Grandma daren't be friendly in case she was in trouble too. The school was now embarrassed at the fuss they had made, as truancy had never crossed their mind. –"Not at *our* school!" So scandalous it was, that they declared "She must not be right in the head!" Mother was even more irate when she had to pay £5 for a child psychiatrist to confirm that I was perfectly normal and it was the headmistress that needed psychoanalysis not me.

The real punishment came when I returned to school to find that I had been put back down into a lower class and being made to sit the school certificate exams again to get a better grade "And this time you will matriculate!" It seemed unjust this penalty for a few hours of innocent folly. I became resentful, politely perverse, ignored all homework and lost all interest in school where I once was so happy. All this proved to be a turning point in my life although it was not yet obvious.

One task I disliked was having to help in the shoe shop at busy times. If I had been allowed to serve court shoes and sandals it would have had more appeal, but I had to stick to the polishes, shoe laces and tearing up the empty cardboard boxes, which I felt was too embarrassing if someone I knew came in! Which they did, a former school girl, Jean, and her mother. "What are you doing now?" I asked. I learned that she was training to be an Orthopaedic nurse where girls were taken at sixteen years old for two years before starting a state registered training at eighteen and a half. With no hesitation, I heard myself saying "That's what I'd like to do!" Mother was against it and put up plenty of opposition "You'd never stick that; think of all the bedpans and horrible smells!" The Headmistress was also miffed that I would want to leave before taking the higher school certificate and stated that if I really wanted to be a nurse I should stay on and do it properly, as other girls had gone to *that* place and it was so awful they only lasted three weeks and had returned to school. "It is a *terrible* place – is that what you want?!" Not to be daunted, I wrote to the matron with a reference from the useful vicar, got an interview at the Adela Shaw Children's Orthopaedic Hospital at Kirbymoorside in North Yorkshire, thirty miles away, and was accepted to begin on January 20th 1943.

Work!

Just Sixteen. 1942

On a cold day in January I left home, optimistic and excited. It took three hours and three different buses to reach Kirbymoorside. The fare was two shillings (10p), they charged me half price as I was wearing a school uniform hat. A special permit was needed to allow anyone in and out of a coastal area during the war, a kind of passport. A small old suitcase contained my entire wardrobe.- 2 pairs of home-made flannelette pyjamas, one pink, one blue, a knitted navy-blue cardigan, school indoor shoes, knitted white polo-neck, 2 school blouses, 2 pairs lisle stockings, school mackintosh, dressing gown and slippers, wellingtons, a navy skirt that had been re-modelled from a five-year old tunic in response to one of the wartime slogans "Make do and mend!", a Breton hat, the brown suede gloves with rabbit fur cuffs, (a present from grandma Mitton) and an inadequate amount of underwear completed the luggage of one naïve ex-school girl making her way into the grown-up world of WORK - and what a shock that was!

The main hospital consisted of a brick-built administration block and doctors house, ward 4 for the babies, and an isolation block some distance from the rest. The other three wards, operating theatres and nurses home were old wooden military huts linked by a hut-like corridor which had ramps every few yards because it was on a hillside. The war had come along so further building was halted, the huts being erected as a temporary measure. It never did get completed and has now been demolished. Also, due to the war, Ward 1 and 2 had been taken over by the military and was staffed by Red Cross and V.A.D. nurses (Voluntary Aid Detachment). In turn, to make room for the children from wards 1 and 2 two local stately homes were taken over, Nawton Towers and Welburn Hall. This, I had been unaware of.

Having been allocated a bedroom "just for tonight", I was shown into the nurses sitting room with its cosy log fire, well-worn easy chairs and threadbare carpet. The

Nurse M. Johnson.

The
Adela Shaw Orthopædic Hospital
Kirbymoorside

(INCORPORATED)

RULES & REGULATIONS

JANUARY 1943

Probationer Nurses.

(1) Probationers must observe strict punctuality. They may not remain on their ward nor visit any other ward when off duty.

(2) No probationer may go to a ward other than that on which she is working, unless sent with a message or with permission from a sister.

(3) Probationers are not permitted to receive visits from their friends while on duty.

(4) Probationers are not allowed to wear rings or any form of jewellery when on duty.

(5) All illness and accidents, however trivial, must be reported to the Matron.

(6) Attendance at lectures is compulsory.

(7) All uniform is the property of the Hospital and must be handed to the home sister by probationers before leaving.

(8) The bedrooms must be kept tidy and all rubbish put into the bins provided for the purpose.

(9) No crockery or cutlery must be taken from the dining room to the bedrooms.

(10) Spirit lamps, movable lights and electric irons are strictly forbidden in the bedrooms.

(11) Probationers may not be in the sitting-room nor walking about the home after 10 p.m. Lights must be out by 10-30 p.m.

(12) Probationers will be allowed three weeks' holiday annually, and such off-duty times as the House Committee may decide.

other four occupants were friendly, but a little too eager to warn me that I wouldn't be staying here. "All newcomers are shipped straight up to Nawton Towers – '*The Virgins Retreat*', which was about six miles away from anywhere. That came as a disappointment – I quite liked it where I was.

Just as they had said, next morning I had to be ready at 9am to be taken in the old ambulance by 'Metcalfe', the friendly driver. Three miles into Nawton Village, and then another three, up and up coming to the steep, tree-lined drive of Nawton Towers.

It was a fine house belonging to Earl and Countess of Feversham who now had to move out and live in a small house in the village. The surrounding beauty and breath-taking views across the moors and Vale of York were to help me through the harsh discipline and Spartan conditions we had to tolerate in the following months.

At Newton Towers

The children at the hospital and its annexes were aged between one year and sixteen years and came mainly from the poorer industrial areas of West Yorkshire for treatment of tubercular, bones, club feet, Rickets caused by bad diet, and other deformaties. Their cure was long and tedious, some needing up to two years of immobilised joints combined with fresh air and good food. The ones with T.B spines had to spend up to two years lying in a plaster shell from head to foot which only left freedom for their arms. They were good at throwing toys about. There were many with T.B hips who were confined to padded metal frames reaching from the back of the head to the ankles, they were very heavy and awkward to carry. Some of them, when fit enough, were able to have an operation to remove all the diseased bone from the top of the femur, and the socket in which it pivots. The two ends would then be put together with the leg set at a slight angle and then stitched up. The child would be encased in plaster from chest to ankle for several months until the two surfaces fused together. This gave them a shortened leg, and they could not bend from the hip. The healthy regrowth of the bone depended much on general health of the child, so frequently they had to spend months immobilised.

So, there I was in a thin blue cotton dress, white apron and frilly cap at 7:30 am (no hair to be showing) a sweeping brush thrust at me as I was told that, this, ward 5, was my ward - sweep it! It was not a large room, just big enough for five high, black, heavy cots like cages with their animals shouting and screaming and throwing their toys on the floor as fast as I could pick them up. Although they were all under three years old, they could spot a novice and took full advantage of my gullibility. Bedpans were ignored in favour of doing their own thing where and whenever their whim, consequently, I was constantly changing sheets, and cleaning up wet, dirty beds and children. The sheets had then to be rinsed and hung in the cellar to dry. We had no hot water and only cakes of hard carbolic soap to deal with this nauseous task – and I had never even washed my own socks before now.

It was a mistake to think that I had only ward 5 to contend with. There were beds to make and floors to sweep in the big wards too, but those children were seven and eight years old, and, thankfully, a bit more house-trained. By 6:30 pm, the first day had seemed endless, my feet ached, and blisters bubbled up on my heels. – "Is this nursing?" Was mother right, after all?" No! I must not give her the satisfaction of saying "I told you so!"

The evening meal was reigned over by Sister Grey, a formidable spinster of indeterminable middle-age with steel-wool hair scraped back into a severe plaited bun. Being the most junior member, I dare not offer any conversation and was only expected to speak if spoken to. I learnt also, that I had to pour tea, cut bread and open doors for anyone else who had been there longer than I had – there was a pronounced pecking order.

The dining lounge was the nicest part of the house. A large, log fire burned on the open stone hearth making shadows flicker on the family portraits and old oak furniture. A threadbare oriental heath rug left ample space for the mice to play as they popped up through the knot-holes in the oak-boarded floor. They seemed to know when it was meal time and ran around your feet waiting for crumbs. If one didn't appear, bread-crumbs flicked near the edge of the holes soon brought one up, and also brought Sisters anger on us, but it lightened our mealtimes.

In contrast, our bedrooms were bare and very cold, reached by the dark and narrow servants staircase. I shared a large room with two other girls - 'seniors' - they had been there three months! We each had an Army Issue narrow iron bedstead with a wafer thin, horse-hair mattress, one lumpy pillow, two threadbare army blankets, sheets and a blue cotton counterpane from the same material as our dresses. It was like sleeping in a refrigerator. Once the lights were out, (10:30 pm sharp!), the resident mice scampered across the bare boarded floor, and the biting wind from across moors, via Siberia, found its way through the gaps in the window frames freezing my aching feet.

It had been a long day of bewildering new experiences, I was exhausted and not only not very happy at the prospects of the same again tomorrow, and the day after that, and the day after that… *Bang, bang, bang*— "Half past six, nurse!" *bang, bang, bang* - all the way down the corridor the Night Sister was rousting us for a new day. Wash in cold water, and dress as fast as possible before stripping and remaking your bed immaculately (or Sister stripped it again), clean your shoes and be checked in for breakfast before 7 am prompt. Rations were issued each week, a labelled saucer for 2oz butter and 3oz margarine, and a jam jar for the 6oz sugar. Every month we got a ½ lb jar of marmalade and one of jam - all kept in a cupboard in the dining room.

Then it was onto the wards by 7:25am to begin the daily routine. Every child had to have their hair thoroughly searched with the dreaded metal small-toothed comb to check for head-lice and nits - especially after monthly visiting day. Wards were swept three times a day, bed-pans and dirty sheets seemed never- ending and many children had to be spoon-fed because of their positions. When you just thought there was a moment to pause and admire the beautiful view you were reminded of the bandages to be washed.

Inch by inch, the miles of unsavoury fleece and crepe bandages rubbed my knuckles raw until my hands were so cracked and bleeding I cried copiously into the scummy sink.

"Dear Mum," I wrote, "I am fine, and enjoying my work, it is very interesting. The rabbits and squirrels play on the terrace and the gardens are beautiful. Please can you send me a hot water bottle. Hope you are well, see you soon. Love Monica. P.S. Can you also send a short sleeved jumper to wear under my uniform as we are not allowed a cardigan".

In charge was Sister Grey, a real dragon, constantly on the rampage to loudly reprimand each one in turn for some slight fault, but we could hear her coming by the jangle of keys on her belt and sometimes had chance to escape. I frequently took the blame for something I hadn't done because it was impossible to interrupt her tirade. She made up for her severity by feeding us well - too well. Being still wartime and food rationed, she somehow managed the house keeping to include home-made ice-cream, fruit cake and large steamed jam puddings. For second-sitting at lunch, there would only be two or three nurses but we got a pudding the same size as at first sitting along with the instructions "and I don't want any left over, I can't stand waste!" So we ploughed through half a football sized pudding with two pints of custard between us. I put on ten pounds.

The children had minced beef, mashed potatoes and cabbage followed by rice pudding six days a week, on Friday it was steamed fish instead of beef, all part of their treatment, a boring routine, but anything different, made them sick.

Just as I was beginning to settle to the ward routine, I was put on to kitchen duty. Every newcomer had to help out because of wartime staff shortages. Never before having made a cup of tea or boiled an egg, this came as a shock. The first task I can remember with utter revulsion is still impregnated in my nostrils- "Here, girl, gut this crate of herrings!" After one slick demonstration I was left to fight my nausea for the rest of the crateful. "Dear Mum, Having a lovely time here. Thanks for the jumper and hot water bottle - etc. P.S. Please can you send me some ointment for my hands?" – I wrote through tears.

The mountains of potatoes to be pealed were almost welcomed by comparison "and don't forget the cocoa at 9 o'clock, and 9:30am – prompt!" That was our mid-morning lunch break. A long loaf of fresh brown bread, a huge wedge of cheese and the thick hot frothy cocoa made our welcome snack. I didn't like cheese until then, but when you are famished and there is nothing else, you soon get to like it. Even without any butter.

The days were long and exhausting but the good-natured humour of the other girls made it bearable, fun and ultimately, enjoyable. Between 7:30 am and 9 pm. We had 2½ hours free time, plus half an hour for meals which we were not allowed to skip. We got a half-day off twice a week and a whole day off once a month, but because Nawton

Towers was so remote, we had to wait for two months and have two together, so for about 60 hours' work we were paid ten shillings (50p) per week. One of the half-days off was always on Sunday. You either had from 1:30 pm free for the rest of the day, which was good, or on alternate Sundays you had the morning off until 12:30 pm, so you thought, unless Sister Grey could be avoided, which was almost impossible, you were expected to go to church. When it was her morning off also church was compulsory.

Those with bicycles set off with her as she pedalled sedately on an enormous 'sit up and beg' machine with all the gears, and the rest of her flock pedalling frantically behind and trying to keep up. She looked like a cross between an old Mary Poppins with her hat pinned firmly on top of her bun, and Madame Arcati in *Blithe Spirit*.

The rest of us had to walk the one and a half miles each way to Pockley church. There was no way to deceive her even when she was on duty on Sunday morning. She slyly trapped you at the lunch table pointing a gnarled arthritic finger she would demand "and what was the text for the sermon this morning nurse Johnson?!" There were two options then, you either choked on a mouthful of dinner or stammered that you had inadvertently gone to the wrong church. (The same vicar alternated services between three churches). That ploy worked a few times enabling us a walk across the moors instead. After that we were reprimanded for not having enough sense to find out before setting off. "Dear Mum, I am still enjoying myself. The food is good and I have made lots of friends. My hands are nearly healed. Lectures start next week so please can you put my bicycle on the train to Kirbymoorside where I can collect it."

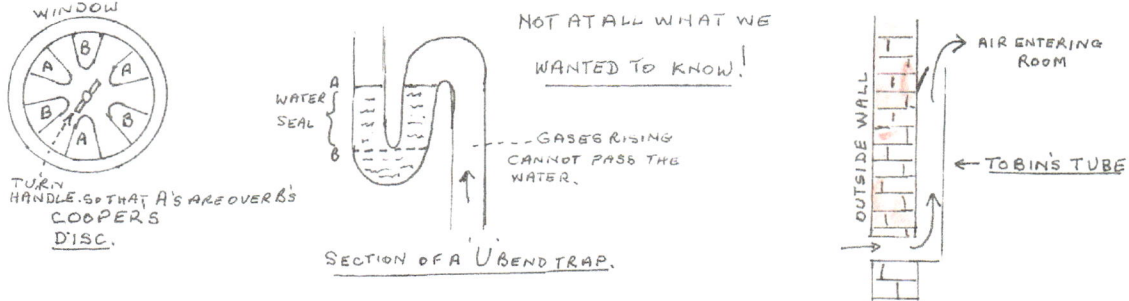

Lectures never happened during work time, always in your off-duty down at the main hospital in Kirbymoorside nearly six miles away. On the first day, we were taken and returned by Metcalfe in the ambulance. Thereafter, you made your way there by either walking 2½ miles down to Nawton village to catch a bus or you cycled in time for 10:30 am a bit breathless and bedraggled. There, we were enlightened to the virtues of "Breaking the seal to clean around the 'U' bend of a toilet," and methods of ventilation with exotic names like Tobin's tubes, Coopers discs, Arnotts valve and the Hinkes-Bird theory for sash windows, not forgetting McKinnell & Shingham! Heating, lighting, drainage and the anatomy of a sewage works were equally spellbinding, not at all what we thought nurses needed to know.

If, after this enlightenment, there was half an hour to spare we could occasionally indulge in coffee and freshly baked cakes in the warm upstairs café-room of the cottage bakery, costing two pence (less than 1p) for coffee and three pence for two cakes!! Earning only ten shillings (50p) per week we couldn't afford it too often. I usually managed to keep 2/6 (half a crown, now 12½ p) a week as pocket money and saved the rest. There was no financial help from home.

The time came for me to go home and was allowed off duty early – 4:30 pm. My bicycle had been cleaned, oiled, tyres pumped up and there was a large bunch of garden flowers in the saddle bag. The thoughtful young gardener, Tom, always found out who's turn it was to go home. It would be almost dark by the time I got to Nawton, fortunately, nearly all downhill, then lock up the bike in the pub stables, catch the bus to Pickering, change for Scarborough and again for Filey to arrive home at 9:30 pm.

For the first day, it was good to be in my own bed and call on my friends the next day, I suddenly realised it seemed boring and pointless at home. Mother was still grumbling at Grandma, my friends were at school, I was lonely… I was looking forward to returning in spite of the long harsh hours.

Simple diversions

A welcome distraction arose on the few occasions when a bat appeared in the hall, children screamed, Sister flurried and we armed ourselves with  towels to flick as we ran up and down the wide stone staircase. The girls with tennis rackets had the most fun as they volleyed with noisy abandon but never hit it. Fifteen minutes of teasing and it disappeared back into the rafters.

Working a voluntary few hours a week came a Lady Kildare, the pretty young wife of an army captain in the village. She arrived in style each morning, driving a pony and trap. By afternoon, the pony had enjoyed the freedom of the paddock and was disinclined to be put back into harness, so we were called out to chase and corner it into submission. Sometimes we let it escape again to prolong the sport.

The most dreaded diversion was one of Sister Grey's parties, where she actually allowed males to attend for us to learn to socialise in a lady-like manner, and she chose the victims herself! Being wartime, of course, most of the eligible young men were in the forces, so her choice was very limited. There was George, the maintenance man who lived in, Tom, the gardener and his younger brother Jim - all teeth and acne, and the two Tindale brothers from the next farm. The elder one was almost good looking in a bucolic way, but painfully shy, and the younger one seemed severely crossed-eyed and moronic even without straw in his hair. They all looked uncomfortable in ill-fitting suits, tight collars and ties but still in farm boots – polished! I once plucked up courage to ask if I may invite the young lad Roy who assisted in the village grocery, he occasionally let us have a cake without coupons, and, at least he was comparatively presentable. Together with a handful of nurses, this made up the 'jolly party', dancing stiffly to the only six records that were remotely suitable on the old wind up gramophone – *Ramona*, *Canadian sunset* and *The Cuckoo Waltz* were among the scratchy 78's. Our toes got trampled on as we breathed in a mixture of cowshed and Brilliantine under the eagle eye of Sister who looked more formidable out of uniform than in it. To 'calm us down', there then followed a whist drive, I can't play cards well and prayed to be an odd one out - that hour seemed endless, but at last came the real reason we tolerated these 'orgies', The Food! There was ham, chicken, eggs, fresh cream cakes and trifles, quite ordinary by today's standards, but a banquet then. Perhaps with all the shortages, the true source of these luxuries was the Tindales farm hence the two brothers were compulsory guests. Roy never came again, he joined the army, was posted to India and was killed at nineteen years old.

When evenings became lighter, a 'late pass' was granted, once a week until midnight, as long as we all went together and returned together. One minute late and passes were suspended for three weeks. Dances in the backroom of the pub were organised by the army entertainments sergeant and were free, so the plan was to ask which one was him, and try to dance with him and ask him to ring up the Sister and personally invite us to next week's dance. If the chat-up line was good, there would even be transport each way in an army truck. Any girl who dallied too long with a new-found soldier friend making the rest of us all late was made to feel very unpopular. Discipline was even stricter than it was at home, but no-one dare defy Sister Grey as she fiercely guarded the honour of her sixteen and seventeen year old nurses.

Spring time

The six itchy spots on my chest showed that I had joined in with the chicken pox epidemic rife among the children, possibly brought in at the last visiting day. I was put in an isolation room for a week, felt perfectly well and very bored, then sent home for one week sick leave, but was longing to get back to Nawton. The gardens and surrounding moors were beautiful and I loved them and became less anxious about going home for days off. Instead, I would take my paints and cycle to find a picturesque corner and become totally absorbed in my scene, then be suddenly aware of a hot breath in my ear - not an admirer, just a herd of inquisitive cows! Sometimes, if it was a wet day, it was lovely to sit by the big log fire in our off duty, but not for long, even that was not allowed for many minutes before the Dragon's head would appear round the door "what are you girls sitting around for?" "Because it's raining, Sister!" "Goodness me! You're not made of tissue-paper, get your wellington boots on and get out on to the moors, it will do you more good than sitting around a fire!" We doubted it but dare not argue. You can actually come to enjoy the smell of dead wet heather and the sting of rain in your eyes, and it gave us good appetite for the mountain of steamed pudding for lunch.

Quite often, in our short off-duty, we were expected to help out at the W.V.S.

canteen set up in the village by the worthy local ladies for the army and air force lads. We served teas and washed up alongside of the gardener's mother, the vicars' wife and several titled ladies all united in the war time effort to keep up the morale of our troops. I was a bit late one day, and barrelled down the steep gravel drive a bit faster than usual. Gravel is a bit skittish with bicycle wheels and I was jettisoned into the air, came to land spread-eagled, and sledged two metres on my stomach, hands, and knees. All that went through my mind when I came to a painful halt was "Oh, good— it will have ruined this dreadful coat! " —another of the shapeless cast iron tweeds. Bleeding hands and knees embedded with gravel I could tolerate, but to find that the coat had only suffered scratched buttons—that hurt!

Nawton Towers was reputed to have a ghost, I never saw it, but, on many different occasions, several have described a lady sitting brushing her hair, when they have been in the sick room for a few days – imagination? We never knew!

Visiting day for the children's families was a dreaded monthly ritual. They arrived by the coach load from west Yorkshire towns and spent two hours over-feeding their 'little darlings' with sweets and chocolate whilst passing on their fleas and infectious diseases, then leaving us to clean up the sick, pacify the ones crying for mummy or tummy ache, and thoroughly fine-tooth comb all heads. Soon would come the next outbreak of measles, Impetigo, mumps and also Scarlet fever.

I was spending a day off at home in June, I began to feel very ill. The local doctor diagnosed Scarlet fever and I was promptly taken by ambulance to the Fever Hospital at Driffield about twenty miles away and was very poorly for six weeks, delirious and a temperature of 106.2 F. Mother visited me once, but was only allowed to wave through the window, it was a long bus journey and could only come on Sunday because of the shop - and that was the only day she could play golf!

Suddenly losing 21 pounds in weight made me very weak after six weeks in bed. I was granted two weeks sick leave. Being now without a maid, she'd been called up for war work, mother thought this was a good time to catch up on extra domestic cleaning to keep me occupied! My long, thick hair started to come out by the handful, it was quite a relief when the time came to return to work.

Ever since I started work I had been putting off a visit I had promised to make. "You must go and see my aunt in Kirbymoorside, I've told her you'll come." said Michael, a school friend. There is a little row of cottages down by the river at Keldholme, a mile beyond Kirbymoorside where I introduced myself to this aged aunt. She was busy baking and rather flustered to have been caught unprepared for a visitor so at a loss to know what to say; but the tea, and hot scones straight from the oven made a welcome diversion. Out of curiosity, her daughter-in-law from the larger house next door came round to see who the young visitor was, eyed me up and down, as she questioned me about her relatives in Filey. This was Lily Rutter, plump, jolly, rosy cheeked and motherly, followed by a very blonde, rosy lad of thirteen years old, still in short trousers - this was William, just home from school! I must have met their approval as I was invited to come again soon. Over the next two years I was slowly drawn into their home life. There were two older brothers and a sister too.

The father ran the little ambulance station that served all Ryedale district and the cottages were for the other ambulance men's families. A real family life was something I had never known, and was enjoying so much that my visits home became less frequent. There, I could feed the hens, climb the fruit trees for the ripe plums and apples and get the occasional ducking in the 'Beck' when William purposely tipped over his homemade canoe called *Mudjikiwis*. Sometimes I got caught to peel potatoes. Even out in the country there were frequent air raids, we were close to an aerodrome and got a few stray bombs and machine gun fire, but it didn't really disturb us, not as much as being woken up by Sister Grey insisting that we go picking mushrooms at 4:30 am, and we didn't even get any for breakfast, but I do remember the mist across the Vale of York, just before sunrise, looking like a vast lake - and transformed into a magical landscape.

Kirbymooreside 1943.

In November, just after my seventeenth birthday, I was now deemed to be mature enough to be let loose down at the main hospital and cycled through the snow to be on duty at 1 pm in ward 4, the babies ward! Thirty-six under-fives with deformities such as clubfoot, dislocated hips, wry neck and rickets, and all doing their worst at both ends. I knew the routine, sweep the floor and clean up beds! A few were, thankfully, house trained!

Very soon followed my first experience of the operating theatre, with the instructions - "If you are going to faint get out of the way and make sure you open the swing doors outwards as you go!"

Orthopaedic operations were lengthy and frequently involved chipping away at bone with a stainless steel hammer and chisel - all very interesting but why was I seeing flashing lights in front of my eyes and a spinning sensation? Perhaps I'd better move back a little. The marble floor rose up and hit me in the face. Having more important matters in mind, the theatre staff carefully stepped over me until I roused, and went back to watch at a more discreet distance. Someone hissed through their mask "I told you to get out if you're going to faint!" Half an hour later I now recognised the symptoms and made it through the doors (remembering to open them outwards!) before the plaster-room floor hit me. This happened every time I went to theatre, even when we just had lectures to learn the names of the instruments. Perhaps the airless, tense, atmosphere, so eerie with the sandbagged windows and sickly yellow lights, was partly to blame.

My first Christmas away from home was more fun than expected, no-one had any off-duty, the children ate too much and were sick. With chalks, I drew all the Disney characters on the large blackout boards and William delivered a bale of hay through the end top windows so I could make a nativity scene for the children, scattering bits over the treatment room and ward floor. To win back sisters tolerance, next, I collected icicles from the roof to melt down for her cup of tea and all the other water we needed for sterilising the instruments, as all the pipes had frozen up that week. Anatomy and Physiology lectures were compulsory on two mornings a week in Spring, and as I was now on night duty, I usually fell asleep in the middle and missed taking down all the notes, which had to he handed in for marking. We were on the ward from 9pm until 8:30 am alone, except for a supper break at 1am and two short visits from the Night Sister to check that all was in order and that you were awake. The rules stated that we should be in bed at 1:30 pm in the afternoon, but sometimes we would cycle into York, spent the afternoon there and cycle the 20 miles back again in time for our 'breakfast' at 8:30pm before going on duty.

Another senseless game was to hitch-hike in pairs, taking the first vehicle that stopped to where ever it was going. These days, of course, it would be dangerous and asking for trouble, but there in the country, there was very little crime and we were all very naïve. Sometimes we ended up in a farm yard on a milk lorry a few miles down the road, or North Allerton , and Stockton-on-Tees, but we did chicken-out after thirty miles with the van going to Newcastle, worrying how we would get back in time. We did meet some lovely people, perhaps we had a guardian angel! Don't try this at home! It is not an advisable pastime! Not even a good idea really, as, by three o'clock in the morning it was almost impossible to stay awake!

CENTRAL COUNCIL FOR THE CARE OF CRIPPLES

THE ORTHOPAEDIC NURSING CERTIFICATE
Preliminary Examination

EXAMINATION NUMBER 133

Candidates must use this number throughout the examination : those who state their name or the name of the hospital at which they are receiving training will be disqualified.

The written portion of the examination will be held at your own Hospital on 9th May, 19 44, at 2 p.m and will consist of one paper of two hours duration on Anatomy and Physiology and one paper of one hour's duration on Nursing.

If you have not heard of 'Night nurses Paralysis' Then I can assure you it is a very real and frightening experience. Waiting to hear the footsteps of the Night Sister coming up the echoing corridor and into each ward, I just put my head down across my folded arms on the desk. I heard her come from the previous ward and walk up the last stretch of corridor, "I must get up, I must open my eyes" I was telling myself, but I could not move. I willed my eyes to open, to no avail. "She'll think I'm asleep am I'm not, I'M NOT! and she won't believe me, I'll be dismissed—" I panicked. She approached the door, two steps nearer and I'd be caught, and suddenly, my arms released, I lifted my head, and wide-eyed, managed to stand up and smile as she appeared in the doorway. That cured me of the game "The one who gets the furthest wins!" and going 36 hours without sleep.

Much frantic last minute cramming for the 'pre-lim' and we all passed. After three months of night duty. I cycled the thirty miles home from for a week's holiday and cycled back to a change of routine.

Isolation again

The message on my bedroom door read. "Report to Isolation ward for night duty - your clothes have been moved up there!" A new epidemic of Scarlet Fever was still rife among the children, how useful it was for them to have me to nurse the remaining infected ones having recently had the disease! This ward was brick-built, well and truly isolated from the main buildings beyond the tennis court. There were only five children during the night so it was not too arduous, but very lonely, as I only saw the day staff for a few minutes and was not allowed to mix with the others.

The first night was particularly eerie, when the children were settled I curled up in the big basket chair with a book, slowly getting used to the different night noises; the water pipes knocking, the wind in the trees and the rain lashing the windows. What I was not prepared for was being startled by a tapping at the window at 2 am. I shone my torch to investigate and illuminated the toothless grin of an old man's face with rain dripping down off a black Sou'wester hat. He was saying something and pointing—I was shaking with fright "Unlock the door" he was saying, "Not likely!" Said I—"Don't you want your supper, then?" He replied. No one had remembered to tell me that Archie, the old night watchmen, delivered a meal at 2am and he always wore wellingtons, so you couldn't hear him coming up the path--- "I didn't want to frighten you by knocking at the door, so I tapped on the windows first" He said! By the end of the three weeks he was a welcome visitor.

At Welburn Hall

Welburn Hall   Kirbymoorside

In the autumn of 1944 my turn came to spend a few months
at this other annex, the home of major Shaw and his family,
they had moved into the lodge to make room for another forty
children mainly between the ages of six and sixteen who had
recovered from surgery and now being built up ready for
going home. Sister Williams ruled over us, a very portly Welsh
spinster with no sense of humour, but a sarcastic sneer for
most things including her staff. She called us all "miss" (with
a hiss) because she haughtily said that none of us were worthy
of being called "nurse". Work was a little easier here, the older
children had school lessons a few hours daily, and a few others

could get up and dress themselves which gave a brief respite from eight rowdy, boisterous, 6-9 year old boys, who occupied my ward. The only time that they were awake and quiet was when I read them a story at bedtime. We grew to like each other! The house was a beautiful Jacobean style stone building with deep mullioned windows, a baronial hall with large open fireplace, coats of arms and a gracious bathroom with a marble fireplace. The family ancestors stared sightlessly down as we hushedly trespassed through the forbidden rooms. Broad lawns, statues and fountains edged an impressive lake, with an island where the family dogs had their gravestones!

The wind whistled freely down the stone corridors and along to our bedrooms past the two menacing suits of armour. Four of us shared a huge beamed room and the dressing-room off it slept another two. We found a little low door which opened up into the roof space, and revealed rows of cupboards full of the family treasures and portraits which had been put into storage. All the intricately carved oak fireplaces, some with secret panels and cupboards, were boarded up to protect them from damage. There was a resident ghost there, too, but we never met it.

Dance mad' teenagers!

Discos had not been thought of, and there was no television, so the local dances and the cinema were our main source of social life. At Wombleton Aerodrome, two miles away, they held free dances twice a week in the sergeants' mess, for their personnel - The Canadian Air Force. Officially, we were permitted to go once a week, but that was overcome by devious means. Earlier in the evening we would hide a bundle of clothes under a bush outside a downstairs window. At 10:30 pm our bedrooms were checked by Night Sister when we had to be in bed and the lights out. By 10:40, we were vacating our rooms one at a time, in pyjamas and dressing-gown, to navigate the dark corridors and creaky stairs, making sure not to collide with a suit of armour. Next, a dash across the hall, another corridor, a quick flit past Sisters room, and out through the window to hurriedly get changed under the brushes, - a chilly manoeuvre! Down the winding country lanes we pedalled our bikes furiously, partly to warm ourselves, partly because we didn't want to miss too much, but mainly, because on most nights we were ambushed and pursued by the village Bobby on his bike shouting - "Stop, Stop, put your lights on... I know who you are!"

The night came when he had lain in wait in a different gateway, and purposely ran his front wheel onto one of the girls rear wheel and she fell off - he had triumphed! Gleefully, he told us to report to the Kirbymoorside Police station at 11 am tomorrow — "and take your lamps with you in working order!" He was now a happy man.

Undaunted, lights on, we continued to a Barn Dance in full swing, complete with five-barred gate to climb over, bales of straw to sit on, and pens with three cows in one corner and six sheep in the other to add to the authenticity and our first wild introduction into the chaos of square dancing.

Next morning, we faced the wrath of Sister Williams, she was not amused, "- Shameful, deceitful trollops, defying the law and the hospital regulations, disgraceful" she huffed and puffed, then, since we were not considered sufficiently trustworthy to cycle to the police-station, had to be escorted by Metcalfe in the ambulance, which was quite a treat. The duty Sergeant tried to hide a smirk when confronted by four innocent-looking criminal nurses, holding up shining bike lamps. "Don't do it again, lasses, will you?" he pleaded gently, "at least, don't get caught!"

An afternoon out

On a beautiful September day, I was feeling sorry for one of the boys on a spinal frame, he never had a change of scenery and I offered to take him down the lane in a spinal carriage in my off-duty. Imagine a five-foot long wicker basket perambulator on high wheels - quite an embarrassing contraption to be seen out with! What I was not prepared for were all the other little wistful faces pleading "can I come? Can I come? Pleeeeese!?" I started off with three extra smaller ones wedged in the basket and three others with hip callipers hanging on and hopping beside me. Pushing that weight was hard work, I stopped by a tree to get my breath. That was a mistake- Three of them were up the tree like monkeys. If they damaged their hips I would be in trouble, but poor kids they had not been outside the institution for two years. There was some difficulty getting them down again first they wouldn't, then one found he couldn't. If I let go of the 'pram' it tipped up with the weight of the extra bodies - what had I let myself in for?!

103

Wedging the handle under a bit of fence, I could then let go and slowly ease him down, encouraged by the cheers of the others, they thought it was great sport. Continuing down the lane, we picked blackberries, another mistake, the juice coloured hands, faces and clothes, we looked like gypsies! Back at the Hall and scrubbed clean, they regaled the others with their adventures "Please nurse,--nursie dear" wheedled three of the older boys, fifteen years old "Could you bring us some blackberries?" This seemed a harmless enough request, so, in my naivety, I obliged with a kilo or so, on the understanding that, they were careful about the juice. I was not to know that they had charmed another nurse into giving them some sugar, and yet another to buy some yeast from the village. It was not until a few weeks later when there was an explosion behind the radiator grill, and another, followed by a red sticky syrup oozing across the ward floor, that I realised what they had been up to – their "Chateau Welburn" blackberry wine had become too lively in the lemonade bottle now that the heating was on.

Ward 3 Main hospital – 1945 January

Forty exuberant, overactive boys aged 6-16 years were crammed into this open-fronted hut, in three long rows of iron bedsteads all of which had to be moved three times a day in order to sweep up the paper darts and crumbs from the rough boarded floor, with moulting brooms. The snow blew in onto the front row of beds delighting the boys if they could collect enough on their counterpanes to make a snowball to pelt us with.

The water pipes froze up, and once again we had to break off icicles from the gutters to melt down. The children never complained of the cold in spite of only wearing a vest and pyjama jacket, and only one blanket on the beds. Lighting-up time was welcomed as then we had to pull the sliding doors across the front and put up the blackout boards, so generating a small degree of warmth. Sometimes, it was so cold that a glass of water on our bedside lockers would freeze over, we then 'borrowed' the stone hot-water bottles and the long thick woollen theatre socks from the ward in an attempt to keep warm in bed. Every few days matron would do a raid on our rooms, strip our beds and remove all these comforts.

I was now becoming more senior, junior nurses had to open doors for me, pour my tea and cut my bread, and that felt good, - I was enjoying life at 18 years and working for my finals. In spite of the long, tiring hours on duty it was always great fun to go to the local dances after work. Saturday night was the best, held upstairs in The Church Hall. The vicar stood half-way up the stairs taking the money, it should have cost one shilling (5p!) "We're nurses!" "Oh, sixpence, please, dear!" So it became known as "The Vicar's Night Club" what a den of vice! There was no bar or alcohol at all, tea was served in the interval and the Band sported a saxophonist, accordionist, drummer, and William, now 15 years, and in long trousers, playing the piano, all young village lads doing their best in slow tempo. It was all very sedate until 10:00 pm when the five local pubs stopped serving, and the soldiers and airmen filtered in to eye up the girls and tread on a few toes.

This Band played in other villages too, and at William's invitation, I went with them sometimes. Kirbymoorside supported one large black taxi which doubled up as the hearse when needed and also provided the transport for the four musicians and their instruments, including the set of drums, and any other 'groupies'. It was a bit uncomfortable, being never quite sure what you were sitting on, but it was worth it as I got to share their supper at half-time!

Spring 1945
Lectures intensified as the final exams loomed up and we frantically tried to swot up about 'greater and lesser trochanters, epicondyles, all the bone diseases and deformities with the relevant cures. Being fairly normal teenagers, we were much too side-tracked by the social scene - mid week

dances at the Village Hall had begun, bigger and better than the Vicar's Night Club, but we were still only allowed one midnight pass per week. This was overcome by again waiting until after lights out at 10:30 pm when Night Sister clomped down the long echoing corridor of the nurses home, rapping on every door, shining her torch on your face or switching out your light if you were still reading "Goodnight, nurse" -Slam. Her footsteps receded, you heard the key turn in the lock of the front door - prisoners! Not quite!

These army huts being on different levels made it that some of the back windows were only about two metres from the ground, but if you jumped out, you couldn't get back in again---unless you hand out something to stand on. "Everybody out!" The first one jumps down, the next, passes a chair down and the next can step out with ease. The last one tucks the chair under the hut. Now there is only a field of cows and a stone wall to negotiate and you're in the street. The locals had ceased to look surprised by this regular happening. What we had not reckoned on one night, was being watched by Sister through the kitchen window as we crossed the field. She was really quite fair about it, she checked our rooms at five minutes past midnight and they were still empty, we were navigating round the cows! At 9 am next day, one by one, we were on the carpet in Matrons office with threats of dismissal and bad references.

Bombed!

The aerodrome was bombed several times, and, one night our army huts must have been mistaken for the R.A.F camp. The enemy plane could be heard circling, then dive, and four bombs came whistling down and exploded in the field next to the ward where I was on duty. Then the plane swooped low spitting a barrage of tracer bullets past the window. No one was hurt, but it frightened the children, and me! That was the last bit of action we experienced, as, in June 1945—

Great Jubilation!

Everyone was yelling, hugging, jumping up and down and crying too with joy. What a happy relief, the war in Europe was over!! All over England parties in the street were held. People brought out chairs and tables and placed them end to end on the road and used up all their rations to make cakes and the usual sardine paste sandwiches. On the wards, discipline relaxed and even Matron smiled to see long tables down each ward covered with sheets and decorated with the inevitable red, white and blue crêpe-paper streamers and rosettes that we all helped to make. Cook forfeited her hoard of butter, sugar and eggs to bake cakes as we had never seen for nearly six years.

The Kirbymoorside Silver Band played triumphantly, if not quite in tune, (William on the cornet!) in the market square, as people thronged up and down the street, linking arms and singing and screaming, too, as little jumping crackers and bangers were thrown, a little recklessly, among the dancing feet. It was a wonderfully joyous occasion for most of us and celebrations continued for many days. The churches were full, as people gave thanks for England's deliverance, but many also grieved for the loved ones they had lost. The black-out curtains came down, the street-lights were un-masked, and church bells rang out their changes again for the first time since the outbreak of the War.

A new coat

When you were on night duty, you worked for two weeks and then had three days leave. Whilst at home, I commented on the state of my shapeless tweed coat and its scratched buttons. To my delight, mother suggested that we go into Bridlington on the bus and buy me a new one.

I still had not heard of Marks and Spencer's, and the only other department store was scorned by her standards. So I was taken to 'A la mode', Ladies quality Furrier and Costumier', which sounded rather grand. The soft alpaca, belted and pleated coat fitted perfectly, so I was told, by mother and the sniffy little old lady with the steel-rimmed spectacles.

The colour, which you were permitted to say then, but not these days, was *nigger brown* and cost twelve guineas (twelve pounds and twelve shillings, £12.60p)

"You shall have that one, did you bring your money?" That came as a shock, as I had believed that I was being treated, since I was not given any choice. If I had known,

I could have gone elsewhere and bought one for less than half that price, especially since the twelve guineas represented half a year of my wages!

The coat arrived by post after I had withdrawn the money from my Yorkshire Penny Bank savings book, bought a Postal Order and sent it off to '*A la mode*'! This coat had to last throughout my general training of 3½ years and the first four years of marriage. It ended its life made into a snow-suit for Paul, when he was two and a half, and then passed on to John two years later! – I think I had my 12 guineas worth of service!

In JULY 1945 the time came for me to leave Kirbymoorside. The two-year course completed and I had stayed on extra months to make up for all the sick-leave I had taken. In spite of all the discipline, hard work and little pay, I began to realise just how much I had enjoyed it. I was going to miss the many good friends I had met and the children too, but most of all, the beauty of the north Yorkshire moors. I cried as I boarded the bus for home and waved goodbye.

After a brief break at home, I was ready to commence, in August, the three and a half year training to become a State Registered nurse at Scarborough Hospital. On July 12th, a letter from Matron at Kirbymoorside said that I had successfully passed the Orthopaedic finals and also that I had come 11th out of 300 candidates - that surprised a few people!

Scarborough hospital

...was, perhaps, even harder work at the beginning - The wards were longer and busier and many miles of walking soon gave me blistered heels and aching legs for a few days. Within three days I was sent to the operating theatre with a patient - I tried to explain to Sister that I always fainted, but got the usual reply "Well, just keep out of the way, anyway, I have no-one else I can send, so you'll have to go!" Apprehension fluttered my knees and apron, but surprisingly the atmosphere was relaxed, the sun shone in through the windows and people moved about, talking. I never fainted again, and loved the drama and tension of major surgery.

After three months of being a pupil nurse came your first 'night duty' on which you had the title of 'Runner'. This meant that after the day sister's report at 8:30pm, you did the 'bedpan round' on the women's surgical ward and any other dirty work that that night nurse could find half an hour of an hour, when you 'run' (not literally - it was not allowed!) down the corridor to the men's surgical ward, and did a 'bottle round', then upstairs to medical wards to do the same. You must not be late visiting each ward or the regular night nurse became a little peeved that she was not having her share of help. After all the patients were settled and medicated, then you relieved each ward in turn for half an hour while the nurse in charge went up to the dining room for supper.

During this time, if not attending to the patients' needs, there were rolls of cotton wool to be rolled into balls (swabs), squares of gauze and lint to be cut and folded into dressings all to be packed into stainless steel drums ready to go to the autoclave for sterilisation.

From 1am - 1:30am it was then time for your own supper - then back to the three wards for another half an hour each - to empty and measure the grim contents of the 'Winchester' flagons hanging from the bedside of the male patients with drainage tubes from their bladders as part of the treatment their for prostate gland problems. The men's wards were noisier than the women's. As well as the snoring and other body sounds, the farmers tended to call in the cows and wander about when they were supposed to be sedated, then become annoyed when being led back to bed, still shouting to the cows! The day staff never believed it when the report read that they were 'irrational'. We had to remove one chap's wooden leg to confine him to bed after a drunken punch-up when the merchant navy was in port. If there were no emergency admissions we occasionally had half an hour off at 4am, not enough time to sleep, but occasionally in spring we could walk down the drive at early dawn and cut ourselves a nice bunch of daffodils from the flower beds in a nearby residential avenue.

The patients are woken at 6:30am as we draw the curtains and go round with the bed pans and the tea trolley, next, give a bowl of water to the ones who can wash themselves and help the ones who can't. Day staff come on duty at 7:30am and we help them make some beds until 8:30am and are off duty and ready for breakfast - 'yellow peril' (Finnan Haddock) or maybe a hard boiled egg that can often be stored in the pocket for later.

Quotes...

A chat up line from the young path-lab assistant at the Christmas Ball - "Would you like to see my guinea pigs?" and "I have some lovely streptococcus virus under the microscope" --- yeah?!

Admonishment from the home sister - "You can take your black stockings down from the flagpole now nurse Johnson, I think everyone has seen them!"

Very junior nurse on an errand "I've been sent for the Long Stand."

From the senior surgeon in his speech on prize day - "... and the nurse who slept the longest during lectures has won the most prizes!"

Many lectures and exams followed with more surprise prizes "if only my headmistress could see me now!" No praise came from Mother, I don't think I told her.

She re-married a friend of the family, Tommy Gray, on April 10th 1947 – another surprise, but they wanted me to call him 'Daddy' - "not likely!" Unfortunately, mother's new-found happiness was short-lived and he died suddenly while they were still on honeymoon, only six weeks later. I was really sorry, as Grandma and I had enjoyed the new peacefulness, and back again now with her misery and anger – understandably so. The marriage had entailed the selling up of the Filey shoe shop and a move to Tommy's bungalow on Greenhill Rd in Coalville and a house was built for Grandma opposite. Mother was now alone in Coalville, she knew a few people, but one gentleman came to offer his condolences – a Billy Matterson, close friend of Tommy Gray, and a friendship began. Spending a few days off after night duty I took the train to Coalville to inspect my new home – it was pleasant enough, lovely garden, but not the seaside!

Sam Matterson

Billy's son, Sam, was also on leave from the Fleet Air Arm, quite dashing in his uniform. We were formally introduced before sitting together in the back seat of a black Riley 1.5 car, to be all taken for a sedate drive to Groby Pool, where we tried to make polite conversation about the ducks.

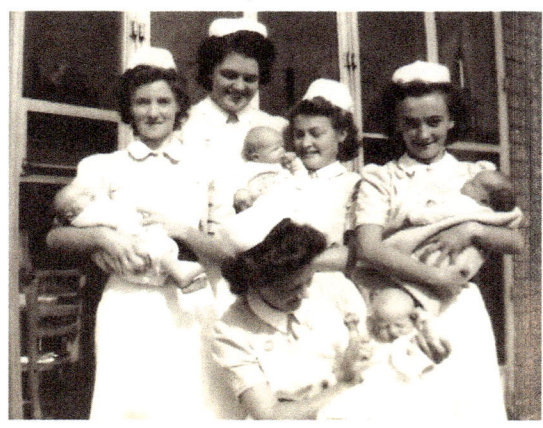 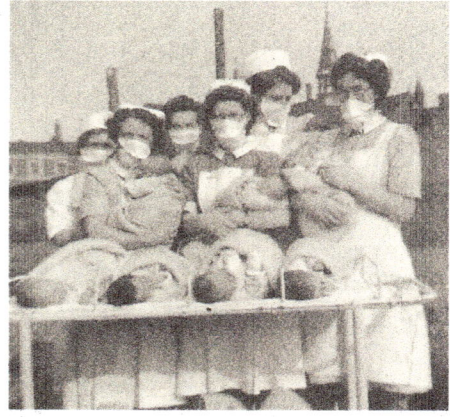

Several months elapsed between our next few meetings, meanwhile my mother married Sam's father in July 1948 and I finished my training at Scarborough to follow on at the Warneford Hospital in Leamington Spa for a six month midwifery course.

There, I learnt the wonders of safely helping babies into the world, how to exterminate cockroaches, how to make coffee in a frying pan, and how to hitch-hike home on a lorry - our pay had gone down from £8 per month to £7 because when you become an S.R.N. more is taken off you for the board!

Sam came over on his *Red Hunter* motor-bike and I cycled so far to meet him. Mother packed us picnics in an attaché case. I shall never forget the spectacular results of a strawberry jelly, egg sandwiches and chocolate cake, mixed with Sam's tie and the cardboard lining of the case after a twenty-five mile bounce over the country roads. After rescuing what was still just edible, washing out the tie and the case, Sam towed me back on my bicycle into Leamington.

It was a most gallant gesture. Poor Sam sold his beloved motor-bike to buy me an engagement ring and I made an unwise decision by not taking my final six months midwifery.

The opportunity of being a Sister in the Orthopaedic department at Leicester Royal Infirmary was too great an attraction when the salary was to be £7 per week instead of per month. That was much more than Sam was earning, and we were saving up to get married.

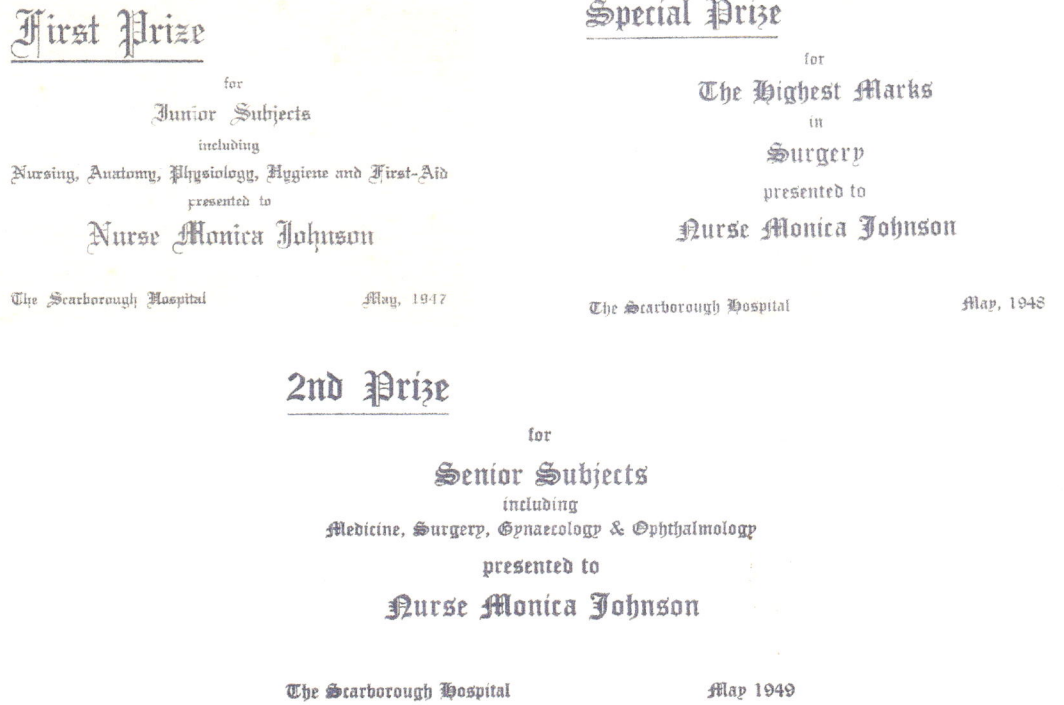

First Prize
for
Junior Subjects
including
Nursing, Anatomy, Physiology, Hygiene and First-Aid
presented to
Nurse Monica Johnson

The Scarborough Hospital   May, 1947

Special Prize
for
The Highest Marks
in
Surgery
presented to
Nurse Monica Johnson

The Scarborough Hospital   May, 1948

2nd Prize
for
Senior Subjects
including
Medicine, Surgery, Gynaecology & Ophthalmology
presented to
Nurse Monica Johnson

The Scarborough Hospital   May 1949

Prize day at Scarborough Hospital 1948

Beginning in January 1950, I disliked every minute; the dirty windows which looked out only onto bricks and concrete, and the noise of too many people chattering along the cheerless corridors. It seemed impersonal and depressing. For two months only, I stuck to it – just long enough to afford the curtains for our house.

Mother bought the house - a small, pretty, semi-timbered and detached one in Blackwood, in Coalville. We thought it a very generous gesture until we learnt that she wanted a weekly rent of £2.50 (Half of Sam's salary!) as a nice little income for herself. It might have been cheaper for us to have had a mortgage, but we didn't know about these things then.

We painted the house. I fancied being an Easter bride, but Mother threw her hands in the air and Sam's father shrugged. We swept the chimneys, tidied the garden, bought furniture and stair carpet - and Mother still protested and Sam's father shrugged at the mention of me being a June bride.

Becoming impatient now to be on our own with a house almost ready to occupy, I met Sam off the bus from his engineering course at Loughborough college one evening and we went to see the vicar.

The Bans were now to be read for the three following weeks and we broke the news causing the usual responses.

The weddings were all booked for the weekends so it had to be on a Thursday, the 29th June 1950. Being mid-week, many friends and relatives couldn't come and my friends were mostly in Yorkshire so I had no hen party. It was not until a few years later that we realised how thoughtless and naïve we had been.

Mother fussed and chuntered. There were thirty guests at the reception in the sunny garden at Greylands, no fun and jollification as there is nowadays. It was all very quiet and serious - I was thankful that Uncle Fred had plied me with two glasses of sherry before giving me away! It never occurred to us then that the short notice we had given everyone had made them suspicious and were looking sideways at me!

Sixty-four years later, we are still bashing on together and writing this book for you. Grandpa has had other motorbikes since and not much frightens me any more except what I must have looked like in black leather on the pillion.

M. Matterson

6th Sept 2014

64th Wedding Anniversary in the camper van overlooking river Seine in France

Left to right - Grandpa Johnson, My father, Uncle Sidney, Grandma. c/900

Happy wedding group 1901.
Far right - Grandad Palmer, Grandma Palmer, Mother, on knee.

Bath time !
Old enamel bath on living room table, 1927

Our gang !
Hunmanby 1931

One of those "scenic" picnic spots on Whitby Moore, 1936

FILEY BAY

SCARBOROUGH HARBOUR

PEASHOLM PARK, SCARBOROUGH.

Hunmanby

*Reprinted with kind permission of the Humanby website
www.hunmanby.com and was written between 1999 and 2003.*

Appearing in Domesday as HUNDEMANEBI (early Danish, which roughly translates into "*The Farmstead of the Houndsman*") the entry adds:- 'one church, one priest'. Found nestling in the eastern escarpment of the wolds, facing and adjoining the North Sea in Filey Bay, Hunmanby was an important road junction for travellers wishing to enter the hinterland from the east.

Little is known about this period, Hunmanby being an earlier Saxon settlement with almost certainly a church. After the Norman 'harrowing of the North' in 1080, Hunmanby Manor was given to Gilbert de Gant, a Norman overlord of Bardney in Lincolnshire, for his assistance in the above campaign. A Norman 'motte and bailey' was built on what is today (2003) Castle Hill. An aisle-less church was erected which over the centuries was modified to its present design. The de Gant family remained in Hunmanby for many years. Gilbert's son Walter, a great church benefactor, founded and endowed the Augustinian Priory at Bridlington. The de Gant's, as Lords of the Manor, granted two charters for 'fairs' and claimed all that was washed up in Filey Bay above the low water mark. The small fishing community of Filey (then) being part of the Hunmanby Manor.

Gent's 'History of York' 1730, mentions Hunmanby as 'one of the twelve market towns in the East Riding'. In 1629 the Osbaldeston family bought the Westroppe manor and during the next 200 years gradually obtained more and more land. This is indicated by them gaining the Lordships and Parishes of Filey, Muston, Reighton, Wold Newton, Fordon, Foxholes, Langtoft, North Burton and Thwing.

Only the male side could inherit estates, and gradually the direct Osbaldeston line died out. Humphrey Brooke of Brayton, Selby, the grandson of Theodosia Osbaldeston was the next in line and he inherited the Hunmanby estate in 1770. He then changed his name to Humphrey Osbaldeston-Brooke.

Humphrey Osbaldeston-Brooke was 24 and remained Lord of the Hunmanby (and associate) manors for 65 years, dying aged 90. In that period he formed the Hunmanby agricultural eastate of approximately 8,500 acres by the enclosure of 1809, making the present landscape of farms and roads.

Hunmanby Hall, built in the late 1600's by his predecessors was altered by the addtion of the South and North wings, the Hall Park bounded by trees etc. He formed 'The Volunteers', an artillery force, during the Napoleonic wars for local defence. Together with the then vicar, Archdeacon Wrangham, a school was formed 'on Lancastrian lines'.

On his death the estate moved over to two more 'great-grandsons', first Betram and in 1842 his brother Robert Mitford. Admiral of the Red RN. Who was the last true Lord of the Manor to live in Hunmanby Hall. A fine man, whose daughter married Tyson (later Lord) Amhurst - she designed and painted the shields which were given by her husband, that still grace the interior of All Saints, Church. On the Admiral's death, his villagers voluntarily subscribed for a memorial. It is 'the Admirals arch', gateway to Hunmanby church.

Now the estate moved to the Mitford family who lived in Mitford Castle, Durham. Hunmanby Hall was let to several tenants, the most important being Lord Cecil who had married the Admiral's eldest grand-daughter. He was comptroller to H.R.H Princess Beatrice, Queen Victoria's cousin and for the latter years of the nineteenth century, Hunmanby Hall played host to Royalty during the summer season.

About 1900, Sir Dennis Readett Bayley, newly appointed High Sheriff of Yorkshire rented the Hall. He eventually bought the estate and sold some parts to tenants and others in 1920-21. Hunmanby Hall was then purchased by Lord Nunburnholme but went back onto the market in 1925. Finally it was sold to the Methodist Education Committee and altered into a Girls boarding school in 1928. This school closed in 1992.

During the nineteenth century, Hunmanby had five places of worship. All Saint's Church, Baptist Chapel (with it's own graveyard), Wesleyan and Primitive Methodist Chapels and the Temperance Society.

There were also several 'Dame Schools', the last operating up to 1920. The original Church school was re-housed in Stonegate in 1905 and later still in its present premises in the 1970's. Land at Primrose Valley was sold and housed three boarding Schools.

The railway came in 1847 and a brickworks established alongside shortly afterwards. Agriculture entered the steam age with traction engines etc and Messrs.W. Parker and Sons built an engineering works next to the Station. Parker's also operated a brickworks and finally took over the original brickworks, building kilns and operating with a portable steam engine. Due to the farming requirements, Hunmanby also had three ropeworks which supplied the farms and fishing industry locally.

During the Local Government Acts of the late 1800's, Hunmanby was demoted into a village, with a Parish Council. Filey, now much enlarged became the local 'town' with an Urban District Council (pre-1974). Development started between the wars and after World War 2, in the 1960-70's many new estates were added, together with many new roads, the population doubling.

Today, 1999 and on the verge of the New Millennium Hunmanby is a well balanced community, still with an agriculture background but becoming more and more a retirement area.

Lightning Source UK Ltd.
Milton Keynes UK
UKOW07f0155020317
295715UK00005B/16/P

9 781908 387929